Buses in Camera
English PTEs

Over Leaf: Contrasting buses and contrasting Merseyside logos at Woodside, Birkenhead, in June 1974. A typically Birkenhead Massey-bodied Leyland Titan contrasts with a representative of the new regime, a Metro-Cammell-bodied Daimler Fleetline. / *T. W. Moore*

Buses in Camera
English PTEs

Malcolm Keeley

LONDON

IAN ALLAN LTD

MORETON-BERMUDA
VIA BIDSTON
22
327
327
HCM 527
LEYLAND
Merseyside Passenger
Transport Executive
24 Hatton Garden
Liverpool L3 2AN

DELCO-REMY
TD.
PINTA
DAY
39

First published 1979

ISBN 0 7110 0961 9

Published by Ian Allan Ltd, Shepperton, Surrey; and printed in the United Kingdom by Ian Allan Printing Ltd

Left: Lowry lives! CJA batch Crossleys of Stockport Corporation make for the New Street terminus./ *A. Moyes*

Contents

Introduction

The first four Passenger Transport Executives were set up, following the 1968 Transport Act, towards the end of 1969 in the West Midlands, Greater Manchester, Merseyside and Tyneside areas. The satisfactory operation of these PTEs led to three further examples, the one responsible for Greater Glasgow being covered in a companion book in this series — *Buses in Camera: Scotland*, by Gavin Booth. The remaining pair, in South and West Yorkshire, was introduced upon English local government reorganisation which took effect from 1 April 1974.

The original PTE areas were based on transport surveys logically identifying the districts which supplied road and rail users to conurbation centres, irrespective of existing town and city boundaries. The 1974 local government reorganisation adjusted the PTE areas to coincide with new, politically influenced, County Council boundaries. In some cases, important commuter flows were thus excluded whilst other areas (and their transport undertakings) were needlessly included. Thus the existing four English PTEs expanded their areas on 1 April 1974, although in anticipation Sunderland had passed its municipal transport department to Tyneside a year earlier.

The original four PTEs were initially governed by Passenger Transport Authorities, comprising elected representatives from the local authorities in the designated areas. Since 1 April 1974, the relevant County Council exercises the policy making role of the Passenger Transport Authority whose decisions are implemented through the Executive, a team of professional transport men.

The main purpose of each PTE is to create a properly integrated and efficient system of public transport in and around its conurbation. Thus is should be remembered that PTEs are not merely bus operators, although it is with that side of the business this book is concerned. Each PTE has had to spend some time ironing out organisational problems and anomalies derived from the absorption of numerous municipal undertakings but the first four in particular have now been able to go a long way towards realising an integrated transport system. This has involved agreements with NBC subsidiaries and British Rail, establishing where bus services needlessly overlap, and where flows of passengers can be better handled by rail. This has sometimes led to the withdrawal of parallel bus services and the diversion of others to railway stations. Such thinking would have been unlikely in pre-PTE years. In addition, PTEs are capable of development and experimentation way beyond the resources of smaller undertakings. This must benefit the passenger in the long run. An efficient network will stem the loss of existing passengers and hopefully attract new customers. The earlier *PTE Buses in Camera* book, by Roy Marshall and published in 1972, covered

Left: It is increasingly difficult to photograph buses against the blackened buildings that were once such an integral part of cityscape, most having been demolished or cleaned. Manchester Victoria Station remained splendidly begrimed in November 1978, however, as GMT Leyland Leopard/ECW 88 makes a somewhat unproductive start on a journey to Manchester Airport. / *MRK*

Right: The associated Doncaster independents Blue Line and Reliance were taken over by South Yorkshire PTE in 1979. Both independents standardised for many years on Guy Arabs which were thus a familiar sight at the Christ Church terminus. Here 'Johannesburg' front Mark IV 7014 YG with Roe body is about to be overtaken by Burlingham-bodied exposed radiator Mark IV WWX 671 in April 1974. / *MRK*

excellently the immediate changes brought about by the first four Executives. We are now able to look back objectively and study the long term policies and individualistic approaches of each PTE.

Many enthusiasts no doubt mourn the loss of so many smaller operators, although one hopes that they acknowledge the benefits of the new organisations. They are not alone, however, as some employees share their dissatisfaction. Municipal operators tended to be conservative in outlook and the change in ideologies afforded by the PTEs' broader roles came as a shock to some. The unfamiliarity of revised operating methods introduced by 'new brooms' is disliked by those set in their ways and, on occasions, the old practices have been proved better. One does have particular sympathy where a couple of PTEs appear to have adopted low standards of vehicle maintenance and cleanliness. It is very sad to visit certain towns and see once immaculate buses kept in a poor state of repair. There is no doubt that ordinary passengers notice the deterioration too and one is certain that PTEs were not set up to *reduce* standards. It should be noted, of course, that in some towns the reverse applies.

The early years of each PTE has been made 'artificially' interesting to the enthusiast by vehicles from one municipality working in other constituent towns. The prospect of large areas operating standardised buses may seem dreadful, but one can take comfort from the fact that thousands of enthusiasts still find London enthralling, despite that area having had a monopoly transport system since 1933. One does not like to mention that, with continued urban growth, we might yet see one PTE stretching from Merseyside to Yorkshire!

The book is divided equally into pre- and post-PTE eras in an attempt to convey to the reader the immense changes that have occurred. In selecting the photographs, the writer knew that it would be impossible to cover adequately the pre-PTE days but was surprised at the variety of buses that has passed through the PTEs. My suppliers of photographs have been most helpful and made the process of selection a difficult task but in the most agreeable way. The writer hopes that the reader will approve of the selection which attempts to give larger operators greater coverage in deference to their importance, yet leave smaller undertakings a 'fair crack of the whip'. In line with other books in the 'Buses in Camera' series, the oldest picture dates back to 1929 — the dawn of the modern bus, and thus the earliest period most readers will be able to identify with.

Sources of photographs are acknowledged with the captions. I must thank all the photographers for their ready help and information, and apologise for not having enough room to include all the fine work passed to me. Other gentlemen whose help and/or advice must be acknowledged are
Paul Addenbrooke, Paul Gray, Tony Hall,
John Parke, and Terry Grant, Press Liaison Officer with the West Yorkshire PTE.

January 1979 *M.R.K.*

Greater Manchester: Before the PTE

Manchester has a special significance in transport history as, in 1824, John Greenwood commenced the first regular omnibus service in the country, between Manchester and Pendleton. Those unfamiliar with the Manchester street scene before 1970 must find it very difficult to imagine the public transport variety that was available until then. The many municipal transport undertakings in the area were adept at arranging joint services with their neighbours and nearly all the operators absorbed by what is now Greater Manchester Transport ran into the centre of Manchester. The variety of liveries and buses to be seen on a stroll around the City Centre was a delight.

Manchester City Transport reflected the city's importance and was considered amongst the country's premier operators. Tramcars were in

Ashton-under-Lyne Crossley Empire trolleybus No 80, built in 1950, about to pass beneath Fairfield Street railway bridge, Manchester, in June 1964. / *A. Moyes*

evidence until 1949, whilst a relatively small trolleybus fleet was operated between 1938 and 1966, using vehicles of Leyland, Crossley and BUT manufacture. The motorbus fleet was standardised on Leylands and Crossleys until Daimlers were added from 1939, giving three sources of supply until Crossleys ceased to be purchased after 1950. Distinctive views on bus design were a feature of Manchester vehicles and the introduction of one-man double-deckers in 1967 led to the 'Mancunian' design specified by the time of the takeover.

Some Manchester trolleybus services were jointly operated with Ashton-under-Lyne Corporation. Ashton had operated trolleybuses since 1925 when a joint service with Oldham Corporation had replaced tramcars between the two towns. Oldham had not persevered with trolleybuses, however, tramcars being reinstated between Hathershaw and Oldham the following year. Turning to motorbuses, Leylands, with the occasional delivery of Crossleys, were standard at both Ashton and Oldham. Early vehicles at Ashton included Guys, however, the marque reappearing during the war years with a further four being received in 1956.

Whilst Manchester and Ashton were the most important municipal trolleybus operators in the area, two other systems had been commenced as early as 1913. The 'trackless car' service at Stockport was replaced by motorbuses in 1919 but the Ramsbottom system survived until 1931. A further installation, opened at Wigan in 1925, was also abandoned in 1931 — just as the trolleybus movement was beginning to gain ground elsewhere. The subsequent motorbus fleets in Stockport, Ramsbottom and Wigan were mostly Leylands. Only Stockport had appreciable numbers of another make, being the home town for many years of Crossley Motors Ltd. Stockport was the last in the area to operate tramcars, the final route being replaced in 1951. Another notable feature of Stockport was the standardisation on splendidly conservative-looking Leyland Titans right up until takeover.

Leylands were also popular at Bolton and Bury. However, Bolton received a large number of Crossleys just after the war and the adoption of Daimler as alternative supplier between 1957 and 1960 added further variety. Bury took delivery of other makes occasionally, notably Crossleys, Daimlers and AECs. Daimler Fleetlines became well established after 1964.

The Leigh Corporation fleet was largely Leyland until 1949 when AEC began to establish itself. The Leigh double-deck fleet had to be standardised on low-height vehicles due to clearance problems in the garage and, at one time, the existence of several low bridges in the vicinity. The introduction of low-floor Dennis Lolines in 1958 meant the beginning of the end for the inconvenient side gangway double-deckers and Leigh returned to AEC when the low-floor Renown appeared in 1963.

The prewar Rochdale fleet was mixed, Crossleys being followed by buses of AEC, Leyland and Daimler manufacture. Early postwar buses were AEC but Daimlers returned, firstly in 1953-4 with 30 CVG6s and after 1964 when the Fleetline became the standard Rochdale double-decker. Some of the AEC Regent Vs delivered in the intervening years showed Daimler influence by featuring Gardner engines.

Salford also had a varied prewar fleet, AECs, Leylands and Crossleys all being received. The first postwar buses continued this selection but between 1948 and 1952 the rest of the prewar fleet was replaced by Daimlers. When fleet renewal recommenced in the early 1960s Daimlers were again initially specified but Leylands had fully re-established themselves by the time of takeover.

The splendidly-named Stalybridge, Hyde, Mossley and Dukinfield Joint Board was unusual in standardising on Thornycroft buses for many years. Daimlers became standard in the late thirties and remained the regular choice, apart from occasional deliveries of Leylands and Atkinsons, including the only double-decker Atkinson to be sold.

The two company fleets whose futures were to become involved in Greater Manchester Transport both specified high standards of interior comfort for many years. North Western Road Car showed a distinct preference for Bristols but during the period when that make was not available, a varied fleet of Atkinsons, Leylands, AECs, Dennis Lolines and Daimler Fleetlines was built up. The independent Lancashire United regularly chose Leyland and Dennis buses until 1949 but the arrival of Guy Arab buses during the war led to hundreds of such buses being bought between then and 1967. Fleetlines have been the standard double-deck model since then. Since the war a very varied single-deck fleet has been operated, notable purchases including Atkinsons and Seddons. For many years, Lancashire United had a trolleybus-operating subsidiary, South Lancashire Transport. The trolleybuses were replaced by Lancashire United buses between 1956 and 1958. Four of the trolleybuses were in fact owned by Bolton Corporation but operated by SLT in SLT livery on the Corporation's behalf.

GARAGE
GARAGE
GARAGE
GARAGE
DTE 328
DTE 326
DTE 325
DTE 327

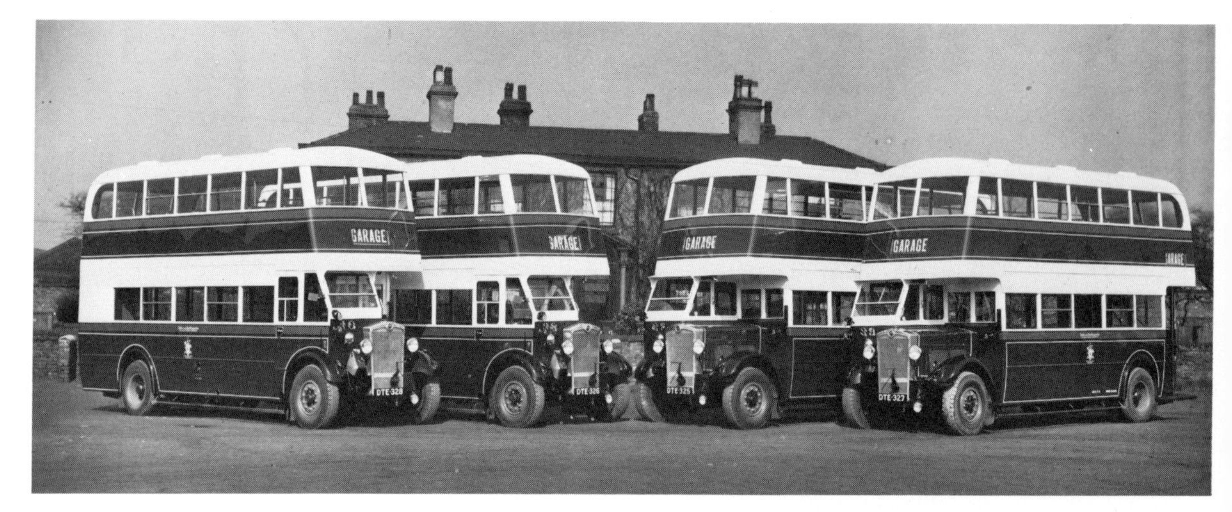

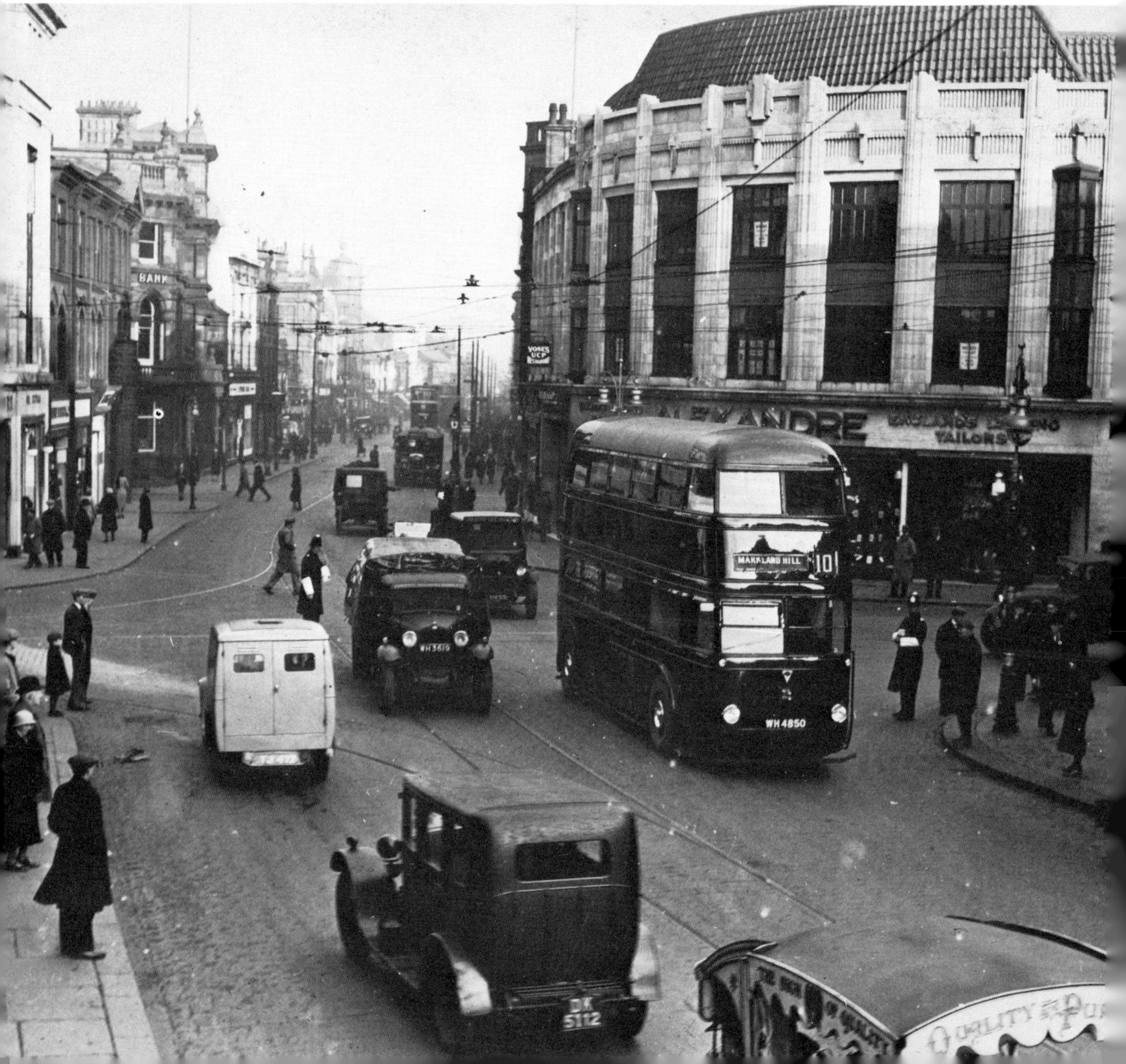
BANK
ALEXANDRE
TAILORS
MARKLAND HILL
10
WH 4850
WH 3610
DK 5112

Above left: These four Crossley Mancunians were received by Ashton-under-Lyne in 1939. The bodies were by Crossley on Metro-Cammell frames. / *Ian Allan Library*

Below left: Bolton Corporation indulged in this AEC Q with Metro-Cammell body, seen when new in 1933.
/ *Ian Allan Library*

Above right: Two Bolton Corporation Leyland Titans between services at Bolton railway station during 1938. The leading vehicle, 1937 TD5 No 123, carries Massey bodywork; its companion is Leyland-bodied. / *A. J. Owen*

Centre right: Bury Corporation received a large number of Weymann-bodied Leyland Titans in the early postwar years. This 1949 PD1 is seen at Kay Gardens in August 1953. / *Roy Marshall*

Below: Leigh Corporation Leyland PD2/20 No 48 emerges from the gloom of Greengate railway arches, Salford, when new in 1955. This bus is an all-Lancashire product, carrying a body by East Lancs of Blackburn.
/ *Ian Allan Library*

Above: Mancunians may have difficulty in spotting the location of Manchester Corporation Crossley Condor 249. Older readers, however, may recall its visit to Paris when new in 1930 with delegates for a transport conference. No 249 is seen here 'en route', in Calais. The Crossley bodywork is of 'lowbridge' specification.
/ Ian Allan Library

Left: Manchester general manager Stuart Pilcher was opposed to the introduction of trolleybuses, preferring motorbuses for the tramway conversions. Nevertheless he was overruled by the City Council. The streamlined styling favoured by Manchester in the late 1930s looked fine in trolleybus form as exemplified by Crossley TDD4 1144, actually delivered in 1940. The body was by Crossley on Metro-Cammell frames.
/ Ian Allan Library

Above: Manchester's Northenden garage in May 1949 showing prewar 'streamlined' Leyland TD Titans nearest the camera and, beyond, Crossley Mancunians, semi-utility Daimlers and Leyland PD1 Titans. / *Ian Allan Library*

Right: The early postwar equivalent of the streamlined body did not have quite the zest of its prewar counterpart. Typical of hundreds of similarly styled buses is Crossley DD42/1 No 2050 with Crossley bodywork, seen when new in 1948. The bus is 8ft wide, Manchester being amongst the first to standardise on the new width. / *Alan B. Cross*

Mackeson
Taste the goodness.
MOSTON
12
STRETFORD RD
PICCADILLY
ROCHDALE RD
15 PICCADILLY 15
4179
KND
940
CITY OF MANCHESTER

CAPSTAN
101
LIMITED STOP
45
SHARSTON
BENCHILL
4456
NNB
246

Left: The next generation of Manchester buses is represented by this sturdy Daimler CVG6 with Metro-Cammell body, delivered in 1951. No 4179 is seen in November 1969. / *T. W. Moore*

Below left: By January 1955 Manchester's Piccadilly bus station was being blamed as a prominent contributing factor to the City's traffic congestion. Seen at Piccadilly before rebuilding of the bus station are two Metro-Cammell-bodied Daimlers delivered the previous year, 'new look' equivalents of 4179, above. / *Ian Allan Library*

Right: Brand new Leyland Titan PD2/40 No 3509 with Burlingham body leaves the reconstructed Piccadilly bus station in 1958. / *A. Hustwitt*

Below: One of a fleet of Leyland PSURC1/1 Panther Cubs with Park Royal bodies placed into service by Manchester Corporation during 1965. The Panther Cub was one of the first generation rear underfloor-engined chassis developed by various manufacturers in the mid-1960s. The Manchester examples, which were 33ft 6in long, had short lives. / *Ian Allan Library*

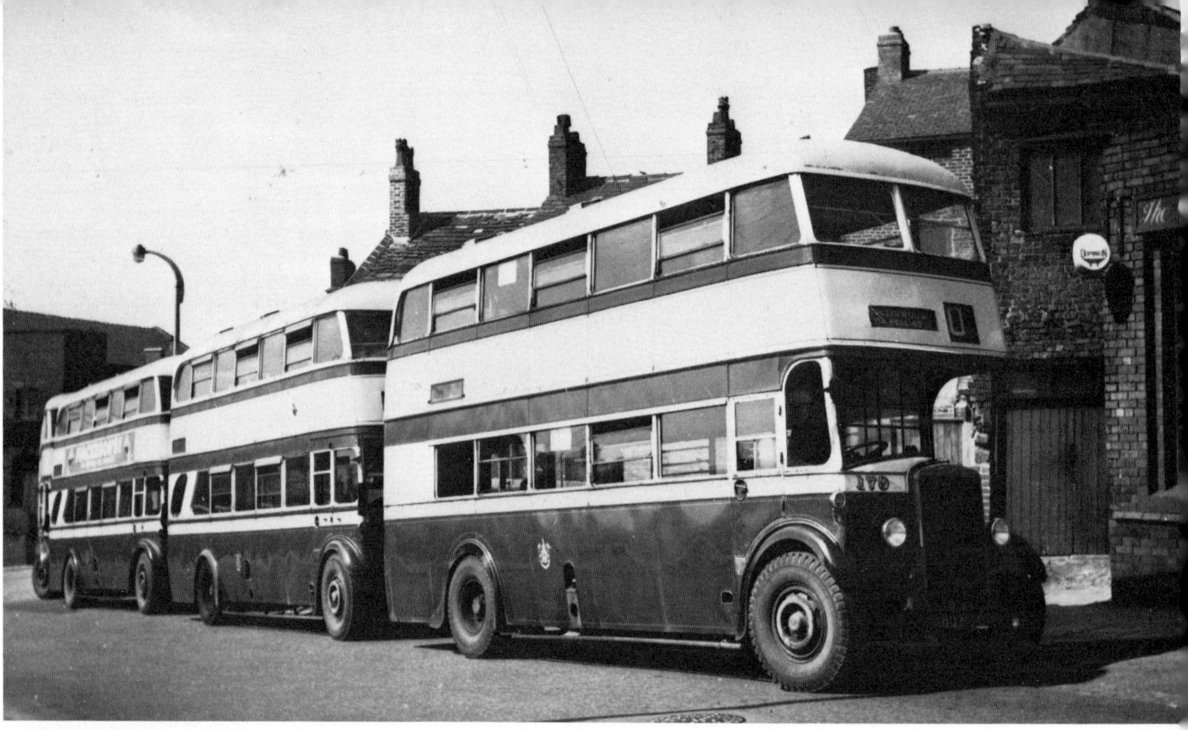

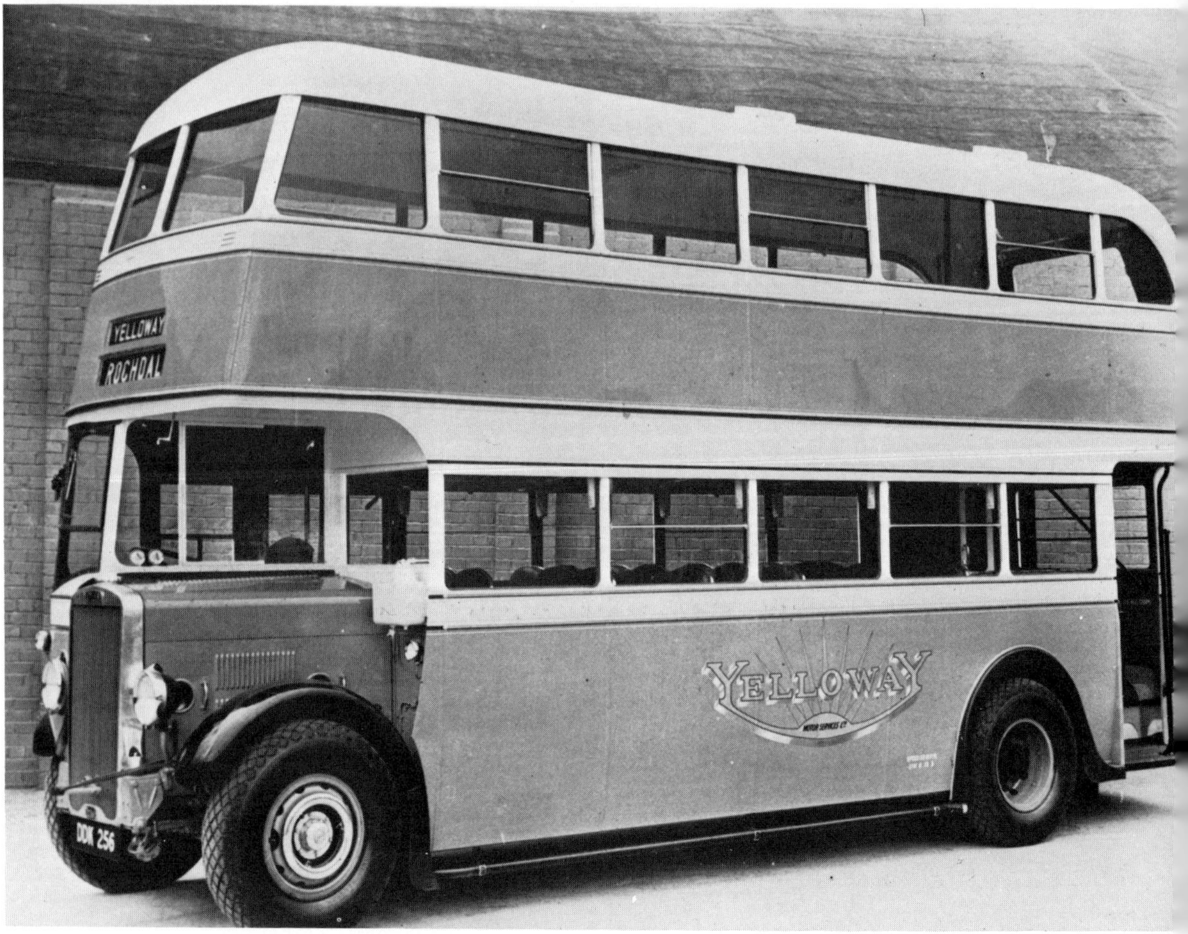
YELLOWAY
ROCHDAL
YELLOWAY
DDK 256

bove left: Oldham Corporation Leyland
'itan TD5 179 is one of six delivered in
938 with Leyland bodies. It is seen in
pril 1954 preceding a line of Roe-bodied
ompanions. / *Roy Marshall*

Below left: A seventh Leyland-bodied
'D5 was added to the Oldham
orporation fleet in June 1944 when the
ochdale-Manchester stage carriage
ervice of Yelloway Motor Services was
aken over by the Corporations of
Ianchester, Rochdale and Oldham. The
uses were split between the three
perators and DDK 256, seen here,
ecame Oldham 227.
R. L. Wilson Collection

bove: 1950 Oldham Corporation
ll-Crossley DD42/8 367 avoids attracting
he attention of a policewoman in Union
treet one gloomy afternoon in April
962. / *A. Moyes*

entre right: Another gloomy day with
ain obviously on the way, judging by the
mbrella. Oldham 478 was a 1952
ll-Leyland PD2/10 acquired from
heffield to ease a vehicle crisis and is
een leaving Ashton-under-Lyne bus
tation in September 1969. / *R. L. Wilson*

Below right: Representative of
amsbottom's prewar fleet is this 1939
eyland Tiger TS8 with Roe rear-
ntrance body, seen at Bury in April
949. / *Roy Marshall*

Right: Salford Corporation 1936 Leyland TD4c No 143 with Metro-Cammell body at Victoria bus station, still carrying the prewar style of red and white livery in April 1949. The bus was withdrawn from service the following year. / *Roy Marshall*

Salford took delivery of CVG6 type Daimlers in both double- and single-deck form in 1950. No 429 (*below left*) with Metro-Cammell body, seen at Eccles bus station in August 1969, survived long enough to pass into the SELNEC fleet — note the Salford City Transport nameplate on the short radiator. No 446 (*below right*), with Burlingham body, wanders through unexpected rurality on the Prestwich local to Simister in August 1961. This idyllic scene of waving grainlands is now intersected by motorways. / *MRK; A. Moyes*

Top: Rochdale 143, a 1938 Leyland TD5c, overturned at Syke in December 1945 and its Craven body was replaced by this new Massey unit, notable for its centre entrance. Like other torque-converter Leylands in Rochdale and elsewhere, an orthodox clutch and crash gearbox were substituted around this period.
/ *Ian Allan Library*

Above: A fine representative of Rochdale's early postwar fleet, 43, a 1948 AEC Regent III with Weymann bodywork, heads a line of interesting older stock.
/ *Westinghouse Brake & Signal Co Ltd*

Above: SHMD standardised on Northern Counties-bodied Daimler COG6s for its double-deck fleet in the years immediately preceding World War II. The heavy styling of the body will be considered magnificent by some and brutally ugly by others. 1939-built No 2 was withdrawn in 1959 and used as a trainer and then a staff canteen until 1968 but, unfortunately, just missed the preservation era. / *Don Morris*

Left: Direct postwar equivalent is 33, a 1947 Daimler CVG6/Northern Counties carrying later livery style in September 1962. / *A. Moyes*

Above right: Bouncing over the cobbles in Hall Street, Stockport, in May 1961 is Corporation Guy Arab II/Massey 210 — still in splendidly 'original' condition after 18 years. / *A. Moyes*

Right: Two of Stockport Corporation's last delivery of Crossleys stand in Mersey Square in April 1953. Nos 316 and 324 were DD42/7 models and dated from 1951. / *Roy Marshall*

STOCKPORT
MERSEY SQUARE
JA 7610
OLG
9

17
REDDISH
(BULLS HEAD)
EDB 570
17
REDDISH
(BULLS HEAD)
FIRE
CALLS

Left and below: Two very different Wigan Corporation Northern Counties-bodied Leyland Titans. TD4 14 dates from the prewar years, the 'piano' front body styling being somewhat old-fashioned at the time of construction, whilst PD2/37 73 was also of conservative specification when built in 1967. Note the green marker lights alongside the destinations of both buses, so that the rates conscious citizens of Wigan could identify a Corporation bus from a competitor at night. / *H. Wall; A. Moyes*

Right: The Guy Arab proved very popular with Lancashire United, usually being fitted with Northern Counties bodywork like this 1949 Mk III with 51 comfortable seats. No 391 leaves Lower Mosley Street bus station, Manchester, for Blackpool in October 1951. / *R. L. Wilson*

Below right: Lancashire United 423, a 1974 Bristol RESL6G with dual-purpose Plaxton coachwork, carried the short-lived grey livery with red relief when seen in Walthew Lane, Platt Bridge, in March 1975. Passengers at the front end seem to be experiencing difficulty in seeing out due to the high window line! / *T. E. Sutch*

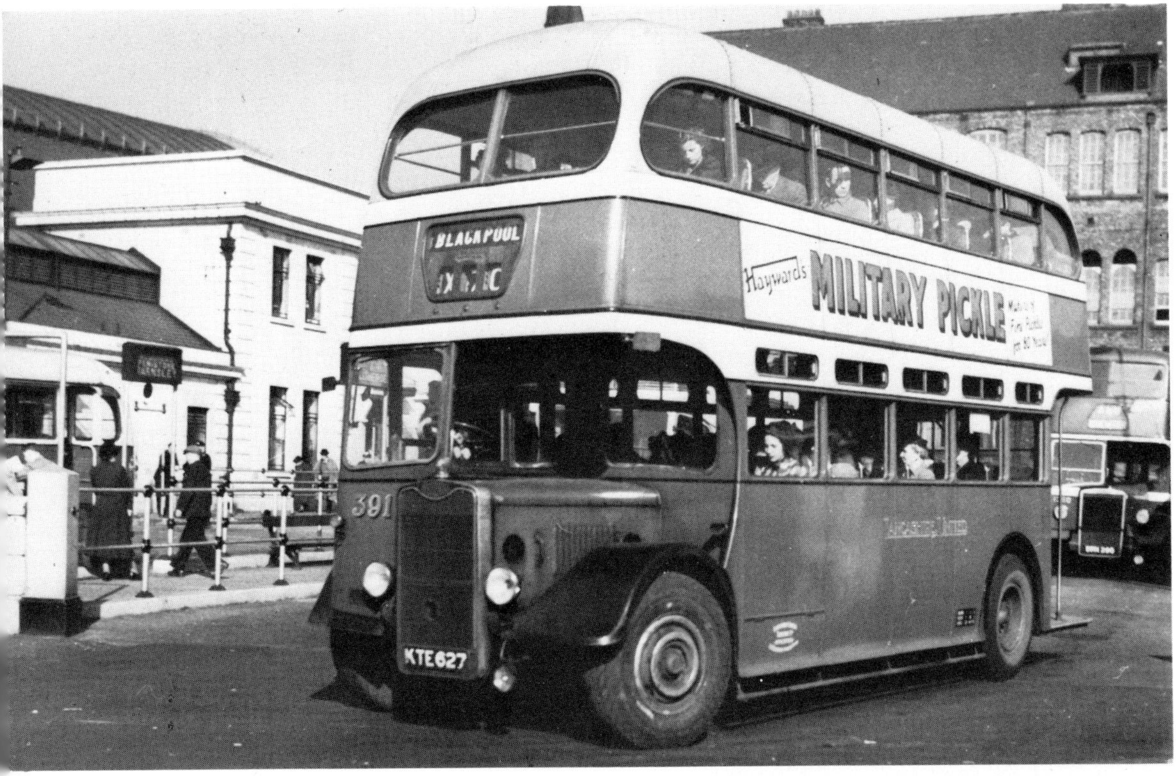

BLACKPOOL
Haywards
MILITARY PICKLE
391
KTE 627

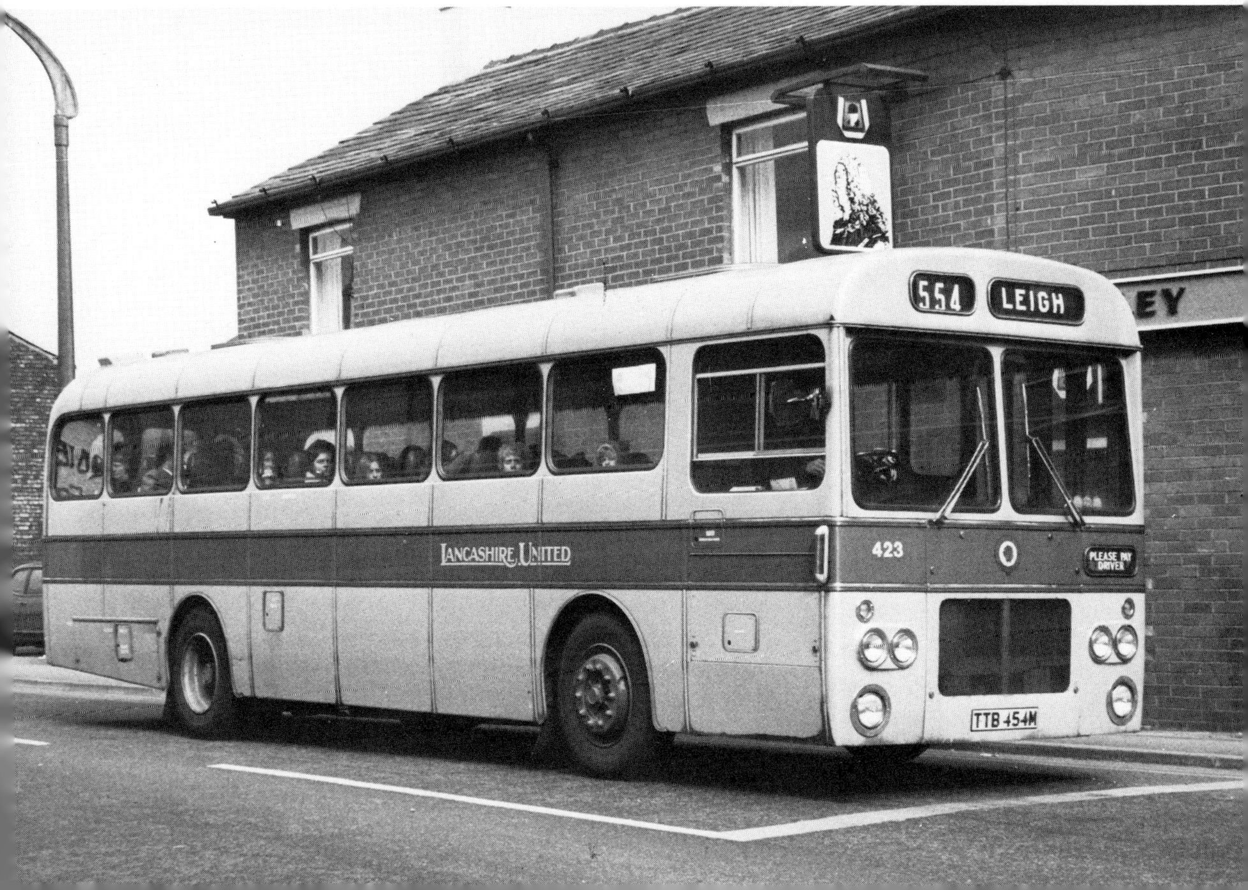

554
LEIGH
LANCASHIRE UNITED
423
PLEASE PAY DRIVER
TTB 454M

Above: Typical of vertical-engined single-deckers in the former North Western bus fleet is this 1950 Bristol L5G with Weymann body. / *G. H. F. Atkins*

Left: North Western rebodied its fleet of 1938-9 Bristol K5G double-deckers with new Willowbrook bodies in 1951-2. 416 stands beneath trolleybus wires in Piccadilly, Manchester, in 1955. / *Don Morris*

Above right: North Western turned to a variety of manufacturers in the 1950s and early 1960s, during the period Bristols were not available on the open market. One of the more unusual choices was Atkinson who supplied several vehicles, including this 1952 BPM745H model with, despite the underfloor engine, Weymann *rear*-entrance bodywork. No 511 proceeds through Mersey Square, Stockport, in August 1965. / *G. R. Mills*

Right: This North Western 1956 Leyland PD2/21 with Weymann bodywork weighed under seven tons despite 'mod cons' like platform doors and heaters. No 669 leaves Piccadilly bus station, Manchester. / *Ian Allan Library*

REMOVERS
PICKFORDS
STORERS
DENTON
81
NORTH WESTERN
KEEP LEFT
FDB 511

STATION
NORTHWICH
VIA
PICKMERE
036
THOM'S
CASTILE SOAP
Goes TWICE as far
THRELFALL'S
NORTH WESTERN
KDB 669

Greater Manchester Passenger Transport Executive

The idea of one transport authority for the Manchester area was not new in the 1960s, most of the municipal operators that were to be absorbed by the PTE having discussed similar proposals in the early 1930s. However it finally reached fruition on 1 November 1969 when the South East Lancashire and North East Cheshire Passenger Transport Executive took over the municipal transport departments of Ashton-under-Lyne, Bolton, Bury, Leigh, Manchester, Oldham, Ramsbottom, Rochdale, Salford, SHMD and Stockport.

The name of the new body may have been long-winded but its initials, SELNEC, had a memorable ring and soon became established in people's minds. It inherited a large and very mixed selection

One of the most interesting buses inherited by SELNEC was this 1955 ex-Bolton Leyland Titan PD2/12 with bodywork completed by Bond on an Ashcroft frame. No 6566 is seen near Bolton's bus station, followed in January 1971 by a 1963 Leyland Atlantean with East Lancs body. / *T. W. Moore*

of vehicles, clad in a wide variety of liveries. To stamp the new image firmly, SELNEC chose an orange and off-white livery that did not bear any relationship to those of its predecessors. SELNEC was split into three divisions and each vehicle carried the lazy S symbol together with the name of its division, Northern, Central or Southern.

In March 1972 the local services within Greater Manchester of the North Western Road Car Company were acquired, together with 250 vehicles and five garages. For over a year a subsidiary company existed known as SELNEC Cheshire Bus Co Ltd, and ex-North Western vehicles carried the Cheshire name until full absorption into the SELNEC empire.

Under the April 1974 local government reorganisation, SELNEC underwent a metamorphosis to become the Greater Manchester Passenger Transport Executive. The new Greater Manchester County differed from the previous SELNEC territory and, as elsewhere, the PTE found that some of its services were now outside the county boundary whilst new areas were included. The buses of Wigan Corporation Transport were now absorbed into the PTE. A new fleetname, Greater Manchester Transport, was adopted together with a new logo, known as the 'M-blem'. The divisional system was completely restructured.

The SELNEC name was thus allowed to fade away except in the burgeoning coach empire which was styled 'Selnec Travel'. This side of the business was expanded in November 1975 by the purchase of Warburtons, Bury. The latter's fleetname has been retained but 'Selnec Travel' became 'Charterplan' in March 1976.

An option to purchase Britain's largest independent bus undertaking, Lancashire United Transport, was exercised with effect from 1 January 1976. It became a wholly-owned subsidiary of GMT controlled through a non-operating holding company, Lanaten Ltd. Subsequent new vehicles have been typical GMT purchases and since 1978 the traditional LUT red livery has given way to a modified version of the GMT orange and white.

Lanaten Ltd also controls the Godfrey Abbott Group Ltd, acquired in November 1976. In addition to the valuable coaching business, the acquisition also meant that GMT gained full control of the Dial-a-Ride service operated jointly with GAG in the Sale area since 1974. A dramatic further expansion of the coaching empire by acquiring a controlling interest in the Wigan-based Blundell Group of coach companies (including several hotels) was vetoed by the County Council. GMT is nevertheless the largest PTE, with around 3,000 vehicles, and the second largest bus operator in the country.

Bus and rail co-ordination manifested itself in the Altrincham interchange, opened in November 1976. Eighteen months later, GMT were claiming that 400,000 extra bus journeys and 110,000 rail journeys per year had been generated by the interchange. To ensure reliability no bus on the Altrincham 'Interlink' services was to be over 18-months-old — a principle which might be difficult to enforce if extended throughout GMT territory!

By 1972 SELNEC had established a 'Standard' bus and hundreds have since entered service to replace the assortment of acquired stock. The term 'Standard' is arguably a misnomer, the new buses being either based on the very different Fleetline or AN68 Atlantean chassis. Despite the evolution of the 'Standard', GMT has always sampled new designs of bus, however. Orders placed early in 1979 were an interesting blend of old and new generations, comprising 300 AN68s, 120 Titans and 80 Metrobuses. Single-deck purchases have been largely Leyland Nationals but the fleet of Seddon Midibuses, used mainly on the Manchester 'Centreline' service, and the experiments with electric vehicles must also be mentioned.

Above: Ashton-under-Lyne standardised on Roe-bodied Leyland PD2/40 Titans during the first half of the 1960s. This 1964 example, working as GMT 5440, demonstrates their handsome lines at Hyde bus station in August 1975. / *MRK*

Left: The Leyland PDRIA/1 Atlanteans delivered to Ashton in 1969 had Northern Counties bodies with Roe style front ends, an uneasy alliance. 5458 at Ashton bus station in August 1975. / *MRK*

Above right: Bolton Corporation received a number of these Leyland PD3A/2 Titans with asymmetrical windscreens in 1962-3. Some had Metro-Cammell bodies but 6668 was one of the East Lancs batch. It is seen leaving Moor Lane bus station on schools duty in May 1975. / *T. E. Sutch*

Right: The East Lancs bodies on Bolton's Leyland Atlanteans pioneered new ideas for double-deck bus design. The final batch, delivered to Bolton in 1969, was the most dramatic by giving the impression of sloping pillars. Buses of this type subsequently moved to Wigan, as revealed by 6788 in August 1977. / *MRK*

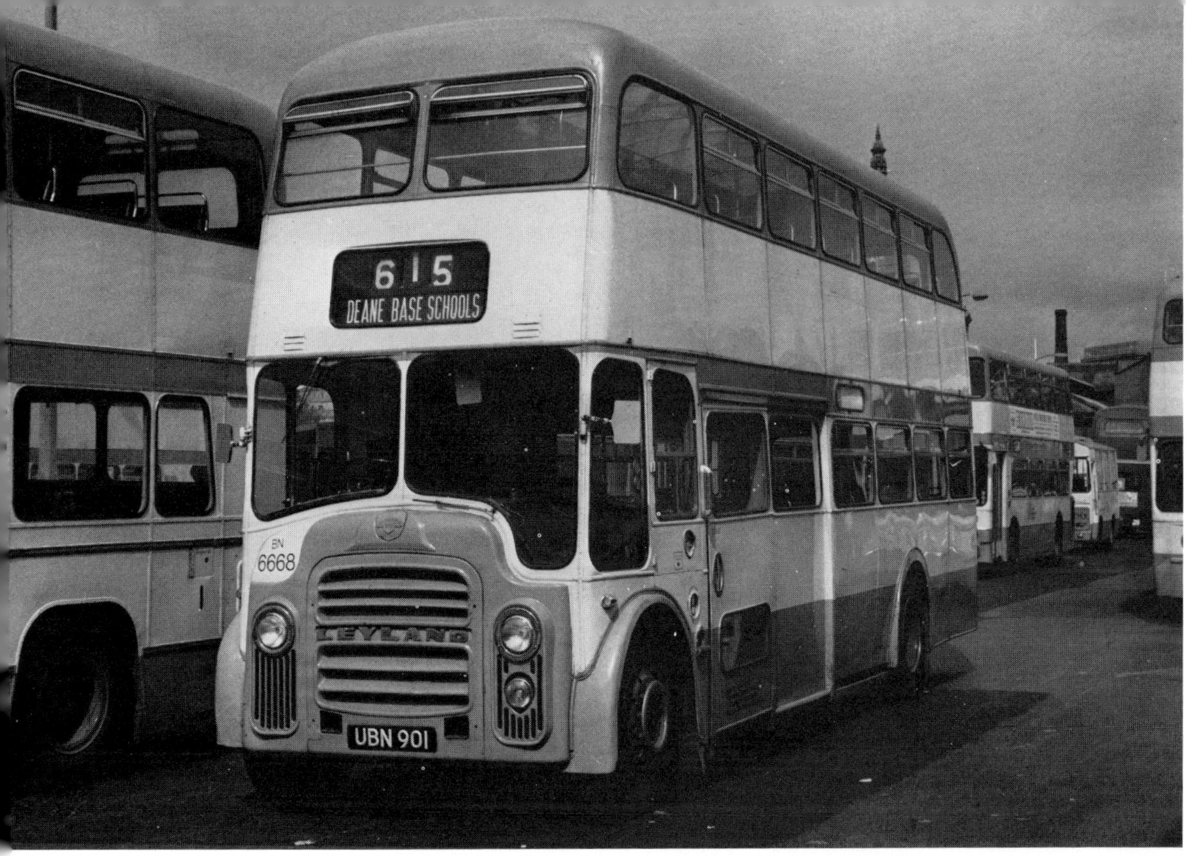
615
DEANE BASE SCHOOLS
BN
6668
LEYLAND
UBN 901

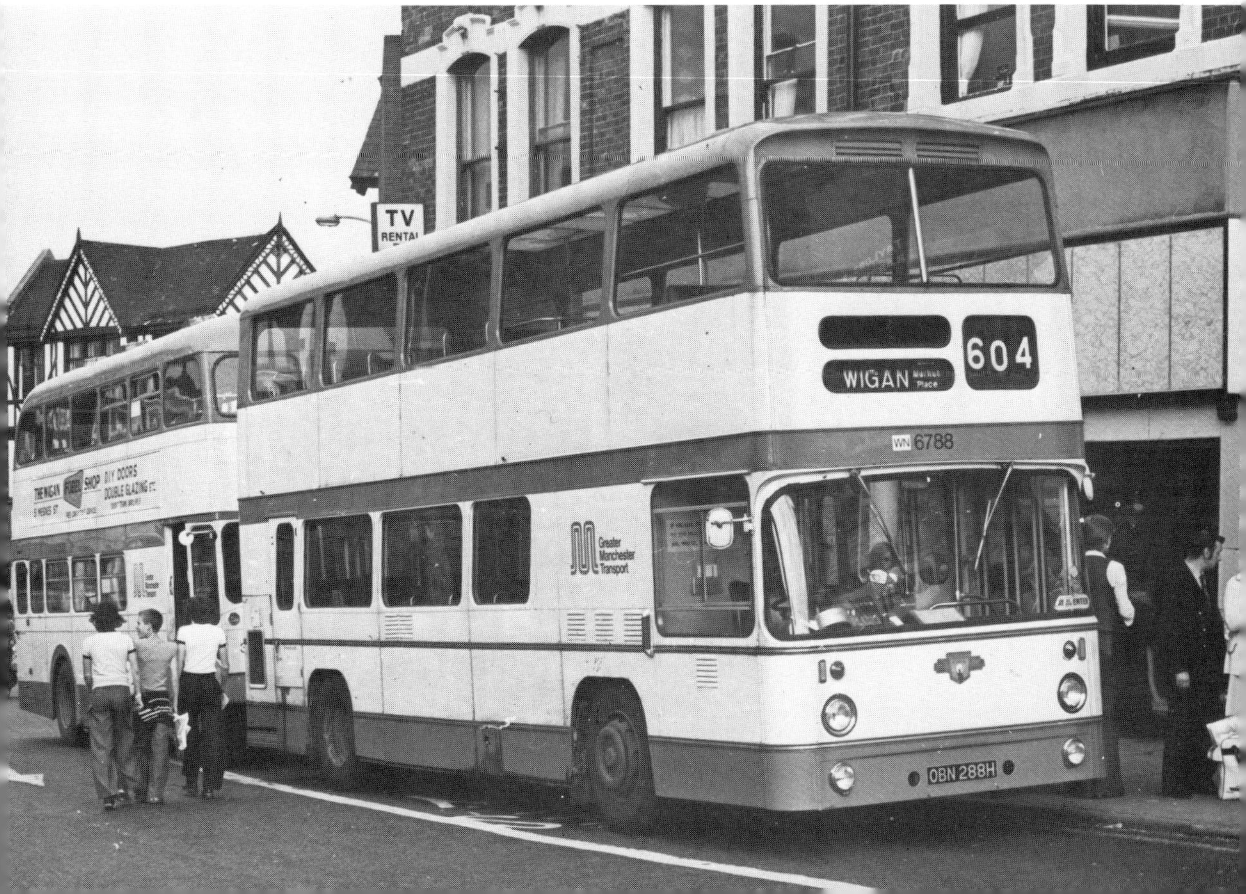
TV
RENTAL
604
WIGAN Market Place
WN 6788
Greater Manchester Transport
OBN 288H
DIY DOORS
DOUBLE GLAZING

ALBION HOTEL
21
via Audenshaw
6386
REN 186
205

JERICHO
IT COSTS LESS TO WIN £¼ MILLION WITH
Vernons Pools
Greater Manchester Transport
6333
AEN 833C

Left: Ex-Bury Weymann-bodied Leyland PD2/12 No 6386, built in 1953, wanders through Piccadilly, Manchester, in May 1972. This bus spent some time working from Stalybridge garage. / *MRK*

Below left: Bury's first East Lancs-bodied Daimler Fleetlines had this style of front end. 1965-built 6333 makes cautious progress as it avoids jaywalkers opposite Kay Gardens in November 1978. / *MRK*

Top right: Bury extended the East Lancs-bodied Daimler Fleetline combination to the single-decker field in 1967. The driver of 6089 squints into the low winter sun at Kay Gardens in November 1978. / *MRK*

Centre right: Bury purchased this solitary Bedford J2SZ10 with Duple Midland 21-seat body in 1969. No 6081 retained Bury colours at Kay Gardens in July 1970. / *G. R. Mills*

Left: Also seen retaining its original livery is 6940 at Leigh bus station in May 1971. This was an ex-Leigh 1953 AEC Regent III (9613E) with East Lancs 'lowbridge' bodywork. / *Roy Marshall*

Right: Some front-engined buses received lettering of this size and layout in the early days of GMT. Former Manchester 1964 Leyland Titan PD2/37 No 3719, with Metro-Cammell body, sets down passengers in Piccadilly in August 1975. / *MRK*

Below: A selection of buses heads for the photographer in the early days of SELNEC. From left to right a 1968 Leyland Atlantean with Park Royal 'Mancunian' bodywork, a 1958 Leyland Titan/Metro-Cammell (both ex-Manchester), and an ex-SHMD 1957 Daimler CVG6/Northern Counties. / *T. W. Moore*

Bottom: An early performer on the SELNEC inspired Trans-Lancs Express was this ex-Manchester 1968 Bedford VAL70 with Plaxton 'Panorama' 52-seat coachwork. No 211 is seen in Mersey Square, Stockport, in May 1970 and was sold two years later. / *R. L. Wilson*

Left: This 1957 Leyland Titan PD2/20 with Crossley bodywork retained Oldham Corporation pommard red and cream in September 1971. 5309 is at Grains Bar, on the Oldham-Denshaw road, then in the West Riding of Yorkshire but now part of Greater Manchester. / *R. L. Wilson*

Below: Oldham's last Leyland Titans were 1964 PD3/5 models with Roe bodies like 5107 near the Wallshaw garage in June 1976. / *T. E. Sutch*

Above left: Glossop garage was the last stronghold of the ex-North Western AEC Renowns with Park Royal bodies. Although actually in Derbyshire, the small Glossop premises comes under the wing of Tameside garage (or garages before the new one opened), hence the TE code above the fleet number of 1917, seen at Glossop in March 1976. / *MRK*

Centre left: Interesting veterans are to be found in Greater Manchester's training vehicle fleet. This ex-North Western 1956 Leyland Tiger Cub/Weymann was enjoying the sea breeze at Blackpool whilst participating in a bus rally during August 1975. / *MRK*

Below: A much newer North Western single-decker to pass to SELNEC was 275 a 1968 Bristol RESL6G with Marshall bodywork, working an ex-SHMD route in Piccadilly, Manchester, in August 1973. / *A. Moyes*

Above: Ex-North Western 1965 Daimler Fleetline/Alexander 4168 passes through Manchester's impressive Albert Square whilst working from Princess Road garage in May 1976. / *T. E. Sutch*

Left: One of the 1974 Bedford CF 17-seaters used on the Sale dial-a-ride service seen in August 1975, when the service was jointly operated by GMT and Godfrey Abbott. The livery is fawn, brown and cream. / *R. L. Wilson*

Right: Ramsbottom standardised on East Lancs-bodied Leyland Titans for many years until absorption into the PTE. This PD2 was a 1962 addition and is seen in Bolton in October 1972, about to make the journey to Bury, where the Ramsbottom Titans were transferred upon ousting from their former home. / *G. R. Mills*

Below: Ex-Rochdale 1966 AEC Reliance/Willowbrook 6027 passes in July 1972 much-missed AEC Regent Vs from the same operator. / *Roy Marshall*

Bottom: This 1968 Willowbrook-bodied Daimler Fleetline SRG6LX started life as a demonstrator, hence the Coventry registration KKV 700G. It was ordered by Rochdale and delivered to SELNEC in 1970 as No 6038. Rochdale, July 1972. / *Roy Marshall*

Two years separate these very different Northern Counties-bodied Daimlers ex-SHMD.
Left: No 5610 was one of the last CVG6 models purchased by SHMD. The 1964 bus is seen at Hyde bus station in August 1975. / *MRK*

Below: 1966 Fleetline 5622 at Piccadilly, Manchester. / *T. W. Moore*

Right: The fleet numbers given by SELNEC to ex-Salford buses bore no relationship to their previous ones — a pity in view of the care taken by Salford to obtain coinciding fleet and registration numbers. 1962 Weymann-bodied AEC Reliances like 73 (ex-Salford 110) had short lives with SELNEC. Not long after this July 1970 photograph, it passed to Darwen Corporation and subsequently with that undertaking to Blackburn — its fourth owner. / *G. R. Mills*

Left: One of many Metro-Cammell-bodied Leyland PD2/40s purchased by Salford in the 1960s. GMT 3112, built in 1967, awaits passengers in Stevenson Square, Manchester, in November 1978. / *MRK*

Right: One of the magnificent Leyland Titans beloved by Stockport Corporation right up until takeover. The East Lancs body of this PD2/40, with its exposed radiator, features winding windows, rainstrips and open rear platform, yet dates from 1967. SELNEC 5843 retained Stockport livery at Piccadilly, Manchester, in July 1972. / *MRK*

Left: Some earlier Stockport Leyland Titans had concealed radiators, including this 1960 PD2/30 with rare Longwell Green bodywork. It is seen as training vehicle TV15 at Ashton bus station in August 1975, accompanied by Metropolitan 1431, delivered the previous year and usually to be found on the now inappropriately named Trans-Lancs Express. / *MRK*

Below: The Metropolitan was derived from the Metro-Scania single-decker, of which GMT also has several. These are to be found at Leigh where 1351, built in 1972, was seen in June 1976 alongside conductor operated 'Standard' 7433, a Northern Counties-bodied Fleetline. / *T. E. Sutch*

Above: Another 'Standard', Park Royal-bodied Leyland Atlantean 7113, working in Oldham with SELNEC Southern logo in May 1973, when nearly new. / *A. Moyes*

Centre left: Looking very much like a normal Northern Counties-bodied 'Standard', 1436 is actually one of two Fodens purchased for evaluation in 1976. It is seen turning into Oldham Street from Piccadilly, Manchester, in February 1977. / *R. L. Wilson*

Bottom left: An earlier pair of experimental vehicles are the Mercedes-Benz 0305 integral-construction single-deckers with Northern Counties bodies, purchased in 1973. Oldham-based 1355 is seen in May 1975. / *G. R. Mills*

Above right: Some 1962 ex-Manchester Leyland Tiger Cubs with Park Royal bodies were transferred to Oldham and outlived the much newer Panthers and Panther Cubs bought by Manchester. A 1973 view of 5001 in George Street, Oldham, with SELNEC logo applied to its Manchester colours. / *A. Moyes*

Right: The oldest Leyland Titans from the Wigan fleet did not receive PTE livery. No 3207 therefore still retained Wigan colours in August 1977, nearly $3\frac{1}{2}$ years after takeover. The 1959 PD3/2 carried Northern Counties bodywork. / *MRK*

Bus stop
5
SOUTHERN
5001
3656 NE
SPECIAL

630
WORSLEY MESNES
Masefield Drive
for all classes of Insurance consult
UTLEY ASSURANCE BROKERS LTD.
THE PROFESSIONAL INSURANCE BROKERS
62 KING STREET · WIGAN
3207
EJP 507

Top: A memory of trolleydays in Walsall. Sunbeam/Willowbrook 864 loads on the upward gradient of the bus station in September 1969 as lengthened ex-Grimsby-Cleethorpes BUT/Northern Coachbuilders 876 picks its way between pedestrians and ex-Ipswich Sunbeam/Park Royal 345. / *MRK*

Above: Varied Coventry Transport liveries in Broadgate during August 1973. The mainly ivory with brown relief style worn by 57 on the right was superseded by the smart maroon and ivory exhibited by 105 on the left. This layout, unfortunately, was subsequently simplified as shown by 44 in the middle. All three are East Lancs-bodied Daimler Fleetlines. / *MRK*

ost liveries of South Yorkshire.
op: Three generations of Roe-bodied Daimlers in the final
oncaster livery, introduced in 1972, featuring the unusual
andom purple band. Nearest the camera is a 1964 CVG6-30,
longside Fleetlines with differing body styles and dating from
969 and 1970. / *D. J. Barber*

Above: Two of the beautifully painted buses of Felix Motors, Hatfield, at Christ Church, Doncaster, in September 1973. The leading vehicle is 37 (TWR 174), a 1957 Roe-bodied AEC Regent V. / *MRK*

Above: Newly repainted Bradford 1966 Daimler CVG6LX-30/East Lancs 237 contrasts with the green, cream and orange Halifax bus just visible behind the shelter in Halifax bus station in August 1973. / *MRK*

Below: Tyne & Wear PTE suffered a vehicle shortage in the spring of 1976 and acquired seven ex-West Yorkshire PTE buses via the independent OK Motor Services. One was a Leyland PD3/5, but the remaining six were AEC Regent Vs like 958 JUB, which dated from 1964. The Roe bodies retained Leeds City Transport livery, to which dashes of yellow with appropriate transfers were applied to indicate the Tyne & Wear connection. No 414 in Newcastle on 10 April 1976. / *MRK*

West Yorkshire: Before the PTE

The Leeds City Transport undertaking was much loved for its tramway fleet and the motorbuses tended to get overlooked in comparison. However a notable feature was the appearance of a Roe-bodied vehicle for Leeds at virtually every Commercial Motor Show from 1935. Roe bodies are built in Leeds so it is not surprising that the products of this builder featured strongly in the fleet over the years. Most buses from 1932 were of AEC manufacture but Leylands were also frequently bought. Daimlers were received during the war thus establishing a foothold in the fleet, subsequently followed by several orders. The rear-engine era saw the demise of the traditional AEC Regents in favour of Leyland Atlanteans and Daimler Fleetlines. A large number of AEC Swifts was also purchased between 1966 and 1971.

Leeds also operated trolleybuses and shares the honour with Bradford of operating Britain's first trolleybuses on 20 June 1911. Leeds retained its system only until 1928 but Bradford expanded its network. This expansion was renewed in the 1950s under the managership of Chaceley T. Humpidge. The trolleybus became doomed even with Bradford City Transport however, the final British operator of the type, the last routes being closed on 25 March 1972. In Britain, this fine means of urban transport is now only to be found in museums. AEC trolleybuses were popular prewar. The last new trolleybuses (BUTs) entered service in 1951. Rebodying of prewar stock had already taken place in the early post war years and this policy was extended to the large number of secondhand machines subsequently purchased from abandoned systems elsewhere which enabled the Bradford network to continue to expand. The last trolleybuses to be so treated were dealt with in 1963.

Early Bradford motorbuses included some Leyland TD1s which, later in life, were fitted with Gardner 6LW engines. The Department favoured AEC Regents and Daimler COG6s in the 1930s. Further Daimlers were received during and just after the war but, apart from 45 Leyland Titans in 1949-50, AEC took nearly all the orders until 1964. A complete change of policy then led to deliveries of both front and rear-engined Leylands and Daimlers.

In the late 1920s the railways sought to participate in bus operation, not by competition but by co-ordination. With this in mind it entered into agreements with the Corporations of Halifax, Huddersfield and Todmorden. In Halifax and Huddersfield, the Corporation retained all local services and the vehicles to operate them. Longer distance services were administered by joint committees, the buses being owned jointly by the relevant Corporations and railway companies (subsequently British Railways). In Todmorden the entire undertaking became jointly owned.

The two Huddersfield fleets carried different livery layouts and, for many years, the distinction was even easier because the Corporation was exclusively trolleybus and the Joint Omnibus Committee motorbus. Three-axle trolleybuses were

Left: Bradford City Transport 1935 AEC Regent I 416, seen in Victoria Square, received this 1944 East Lancs body as replacement for its original English Electric one. / *R. F. Mack*

favoured in Huddersfield, Karriers before the war changing to Sunbeams and BUTs postwar. The last trolleybuses delivered in 1959 were Britain's last six-wheelers. The system was replaced between 1961 and 1968. In the motorbus line, some prewar AECs were notable in being fitted from new with Gardner 6LW engines. AECs remained popular until the 1960s when, after a brief Leyland period, Daimlers became standard. Seddon RU single-deckers were unusual purchases in the seventies.

The railway interests in the joint committees were passed under the 1968 Transport Act to the National Bus Company subsidiary, Amalgamated Passenger Transport Ltd. The Huddersfield joint committee disappeared soon after when the Corporation purchased the NBC interests.

Big-engined AECs were popular, and necessary, in Halifax before the war but here the 8.8 litre engine was preferred. After the war, AEC Regents were joined by Leyland Titans and Daimlers, including some of the rare CD650 models. Daimler Fleetlines were standard from 1966. Single-deck buying included Albion Nimbuses and several secondhand buses and coaches, a number of the latter receiving new coach bodies in the 1960s at a time when rebodying was unfashionable.

The relatively small Todmorden JOC undertaking was a staunch Leyland user. Standardisation on double-deckers was achieved just after the war, single-deckers not returning until a complete change of policy in 1961. In the next 10 years, secondhand single-deckers assisted the intake of new Leopards to speed the conversion of services to one-man operation.

As mentioned earlier the rail interests in Halifax and Todmorden JOC were transferred to Amalgamated Passenger Transport Ltd. Early in 1971 most services of Hebble Motor Services, another NBC subsidiary, logically passed to Halifax JOC echoing an earlier arrangement when in 1929 the Halifax local services of Hebble, on acquisition by the LMS railway, had passed to the new JOC. Further integration occurred later in 1971 when Todmorden JOC and the newly enlarged Halifax JOC were merged to form the Calderdale Joint Omnibus Committee. Amalgamated Passenger Transport Ltd retained its interest until the formation of West Yorkshire PTE on 1 April 1974.

Below left: Snow highlights trolleybus wires normally lost against sooty buildings. The advertisement on the side of Bradford 1934 AEC 661T 603 sounds a tempting proposition one disgusting day in February 1954. The trolleybus had been rebodied by Northern Coachbuilders in 1949. / *Roy Marshall*

Below: Another rebodied Bradford vehicle, this prewar AEC 661T trolleybus received the Crossley body shown in 1952. Most appropriately 635 is overtaking a Bradford van. / *S. E. Letts*

Left: New Bradford Daimler CVD6/Brush 549 loads at the height of the immediate postwar travel boom, in June 1948. / *Roy Marshall*

Below: Originally starting life in 1944 as a Darlington Corporation single-deck trolleybus, this Karrier W entered service as Bradford 792 in 1958 with the new East Lancs body shown. Across the road is an indigenous Karrier W, 709, rebodied by East Lancs two years later. Behind the trolleyscape, the familiar tower of City Hall. / *T. W. Moore*

Left: Halifax standardised on 8.8 litre-engine AEC Regents in the years immediately preceding World War II, usually with timber-framed bodies by Park Royal or Roe. Bus 45, seen here in August 1948, has a body by the former. / *Roy Marshall*

Below: In complete contrast were the 10 Albion Nimbus NS3AN models with Weymann 31-seat bodies purchased in 1963. No 258 is seen at Halifax bus station in October of that year. The Mill Bank service was later to be (mostly) absorbed in an ex-Hebble route by Calderdale. / *A. Moyes*

Bottom: West Yorkshire PTE still operates service 28 to Rochdale, enabling buses of that undertaking to be seen alongside those of Greater Manchester PTE. Hebble 60, a 1953 Weymann-bodied Leyland Royal Tiger, is a reminder of an earlier era. / *S. E. Letts*

4bove: Todmorden Joint Omnibus Committee was 100% double-deck for nany years. 1962 Leyland Leopard/East Lancs 16 was one of the first single-deckers after their reintroduction. Note both the Corporation coat-of-arms and BR symbol on the side of 16 in this April 1968 view at Todmorden bus station. This bus became Calderdale 335 n 1971 and West Yorkshire PTE 3335 in 1974. / *R. L. Wilson*

Centre right: This veteran Leyland-bodied Leyland Titan PD2/1 was already 21 years old when seen at Todmorden during July 1971, carrying fleet number 351 in the newly-formed Calderdale undertaking. Not surprisingly it did not survive long enough to shed its Todmorden dark green and cream livery n favour of Calderdale colours, although a pair of its slightly newer PD2/12 brothers did. / *MRK*

Bottom right: Anxious to commence withdrawal of its 1960 Regent Vs, Calderdale purchased four 1956 AEC Regent V/Park Royal buses from Maidstone & District as a stopgap measure. They were not repainted, the M&D livery fortunately approximating to the former Todmorden colours. No 362 storms into Burnley bus station in July 1972 before making a journey across the Pennines towards Leeds. / *MRK*

Right: Two Huddersfield JOC snout-fronted AEC Regents in splendid condition in September 1947. The leading vehicle, 141, dates from 1938 and has Park Royal metal-framed bodywork; its companion (133) is a year older and is Brush-bodied. / *R. A. Mills*

Below: Big front-entrance Daimlers with Gardner 6LX engines eventually became popular in the two Huddersfield fleets. Left to right, JOC bus 117 and Corporation 446 carry Roe bodies, whilst Corporation 459 has a Neepsend body. The three date from 1965-6, note the different liveries applied to JOC and Corporation buses. / *T. W. Moore*

Left: Huddersfield Corporation 544, a 1947 Karrier MS2 with Park Royal 70-seat body, pauses whilst lowbridge 1954 AEC Regent/East Lancs 237 clears the junction. The three-window layout at the front of the upper deck was a feature of Huddersfield trolleybuses until the 1950s. / *C. B. Golding*

Below: Huddersfield took delivery of its first batch of Seddon RUs with Seddon bodies in 1970. No 32 is seen en route for Stocksmoor in August of that year. / *T. W. Moore*

Above: The streamlining fad was at its height when this Leeds City Transport AEC Regent was exhibited at the 1935 Commercial Motor Show. The body for No 200 was a one-off product, standard bodies for Leeds being considerably more restrained. The bus looks more depressed than streamlined! It was subsequently rebuilt to half cab. / *AEC*

Right: Roe bodies for Leeds in the 1932-5 period were of this general appearance. This 1934 example is one of a number reconditioned just after the war to extend its lifespan. The rebuilding was to such good effect that some were transferred to wartime Daimlers when their austerity bodies wore out. 1945 CWA6 78 is seen at Leeds bus station in October 1956. / *Roy Marshall*

Top right: Leeds City Transport took delivery of 20 all-Crossley DD42/7 models in 1949. No 705 is seen near the bus station. / *R. F. Mack*

Centre right: The then tiny Leeds single-deck fleet received eight new underfloor-engined vehicles in 1954-5. The centre-entrance Roe bodies accommodated 34 seated and 28 standing passengers. The industry was just getting over an inexplicable phase of 'crush-load' single-deckers for which underfloor-engined vehicles with their high floor line were completely unsuited. Leeds was obviously testing the market as the eight included three different manufacturers, AEC, Guy and Leyland. No 34 was an AEC Reliance and was exhibited at the 1954 Commercial Motor Show. / *Ian Allan Library*

Below: Leeds reverted to classic open-platform rear-entrance double-deckers with 'easy change' gearboxes until settling into the rear-engine era during the 1960s. No 283, a 1958 Leyland PD3/5, and 969, a 1965 AEC Regent V, both with Roe bodies, represent these fine buses. / *T. W. Moore*

CHAM
GLASGOW
UNITED SERVICES
OLD BRODSWORTH. HOOTON PAGNEL
SOUTH ELMSALL. HEMSWORTH.
WAKEFIELD.
UNITED SERVICE
CWX 521

BADDELEY BROS
LTD. DEEPCAR

Top left: By the time United Services passed to West Yorkshire PTE in 1977, the business was entirely in the hands of W. R. and P. Bingley Ltd. One of the earlier partners, however, was W. Everett, taken over by Bingley in 1969. Everett bought new this Dennis-bodied Dennis Lancet in 1938 seen at Doncaster Marsh Gate bus station in September 1949. / *Roy Marshall*

Left: Baddeley Bros, of Holmfirth was purchased by West Yorkshire PTE in 1976. This former Leigh Corporation 1938 Leyland TD5 with Massey body, DTD 169, seen at Huddersfield bus station on a short working to Deepcar in July 1966, was withdrawn many years before the takeover. / *Roy Marshall*

Above: Huddersfield took over the stage carriage services of Hanson's in 1969, a process completed by the PTE when it acquired the coaching business in 1974. Hanson 236 was a 1947 Albion Valkyrie with Burlingham bus bodywork. / *Roy Marshall*

Right: The services of two Wallace Arnold stage carriage subsidiaries, Farsley Omnibus and Kippax, passed to Leeds City Transport in March 1968. For many years both subsidiaries operated former Wallace Arnold Daimler coaches fitted with new Roe double-deck bodies. MUB 433 thus commenced life in 1949 as a coach, entering Farsley service with this Roe body in 1957. It is seen at Pudsey in February 1968. / *Roy Marshall*

West Yorkshire Passenger Transport Executive

Formed in April 1974, the West Yorkshire PTE serves the largest metropolitan county in geographical terms, an area of 780 square miles.

Initially the Executive took over the municipal transport undertakings of the old Bradford, Leeds, Huddersfield and Halifax councils including the Calderdale services, and the interests of the non-operating NBC holding company, Amalgamated Passenger Transport Ltd. Four operating districts correspond to four of the District Councils, namely Bradford, Leeds, Kirklees and Calderdale. The headquarters of the PTE was set up, however, in Wakefield, a NBC stronghold with little direct PTE operating influence. The Executive has since acquired the contract, private hire and licensed operations of other smaller operators. These were

Low-height Northern Counties-bodied Fleetline 7008 at Halifax in August 1977. / *MRK*

Hanson Coach Service Ltd of Huddersfield; Baddeley Bros Ltd of Holmfirth and W. R. and P. Bingley Ltd of Kinsley, near Pontefract. These acquisitions took place in 1974, 1976 and 1977 respectively, the last providing the PTE with a service in Wakefield. They continued to trade as separate coaching units until 1979 when Hansons and Baddeleys were sold off following considerable losses.

Negotiations with the NBC culminated in the formation of the Metro-National Transport Company in January 1978, thus bringing almost all stage carriage operations in West Yorkshire under the umbrella of one organisation. Local rail services were brought within the full jurisdiction of the Executive from 1 January 1979.

The original proposal to paint buses in a different colour for each district was not proceeded with, vehicles receiving instead a standard livery of Verona green and buttermilk. Vehicles inherited from municipal undertakings have swapped districts, often assisting type standardisation in their new homes.

New buses have generally been Atlanteans or Fleetlines with a standard style of Roe body. A few Fleetlines have low-height Northern Counties bodies. However a large number of Metropolitans has also been bought, together with single examples of the Ailsa and Foden. Like many other operators, the PTE is to evaluate both Leyland Titans and MCW Metrobuses for future fleet requirements. In the single-deck line, several batches of Bristol LHS and Leyland Leopard models have been taken — West Yorkshire being alone amongst PTEs in standardising on Leopards for larger single-deckers. The coach fleets featured Fords and Volvo B58s.

The Executive controls the £16m Bradford bus/rail interchange, opened for operation in March 1977. The concept of the interchange was initially that of Bradford Corporation. The entire bus station is covered and is used by many PTE and NBC services, including long distance express coaches. Beneath the bus station is a garage for 200 PTE buses which has enabled the closure of five ex-Bradford garages. An eight-storey block includes offices for the Bradford District of the PTE and the NBC, and full facilities for platform staff. The massive complex incorporates a number of outstanding engineering and constructional features and was commended in the *Financial Times* Industrial Architecture Award 1978.

Right: This 1963 AEC Regent V/Metro-Cammell looked little different from its Bradford City Transport days when seen in 1974. / *John Fozard*

80
BANKFOOT
HEATON
Metro Bradford
LAK 301G
Brown Muffs

HIGHROAD WELL
Town Centre
Wheatley
11
25
MJX 25

Top left: This late-model (1968) Leyland Titan PD3A/12 with Alexander body is unusual in displaying the Metro fleetname whilst retaining Bradford colours. / *John Fozard*

Below left: A number of experimental liveries were tried immediately before and after the formation of the West Yorkshire PTE in 1974. Ex-Halifax 25, a 1960 MCW-bodied Leyland PD2/37, received this dark green and cream livery, featuring red wheels. Note the unusual fleetname treatment. The bus became 3025 in the PTE stock list. / *John Fozard*

Three views taken at Halifax bus station in March 1975 give some indication of the variety of buses taken over by the West Yorkshire Passenger Transport Executive.
Above: No 2413 is one of the Daimler Fleetlines with very tall-looking Alexander bodies delivered to Bradford in 1970.

Centre left: No 3215, a late survivor of a batch of 1960 AEC Regent V/MCW buses from the Calderdale fleet.

Bottom left: This 1961 Leyland Titan PD3A/2 with Roe body was one of Huddersfield Corporation's first batch of trolleybus replacement vehicles. No 4402 prepares to return to its town of origin. / *Roy Marshall*

SWARCLIFFE
23
LEEDS CITY
TRANSPORT
115
LNW
FURNITURE
IGFA

401 CENTRAL BUS STN
LCT
406D
33
LEEDS
YUA 533J

Left: Buses continued to run with old fleetnames for some years. No 115, delivered in 1964, was the last of many Roe-bodied Daimler CVG6LX-30 buses supplied to Leeds. It is seen in the City Centre in June 1975. / *T. E. Sutch*

Below left: The other extreme in Leeds vehicle sizes — one of a batch of Mercedes-Benz L406D minibuses bought in 1970 for a City Centre service. No 33 is seen in the second, lighter, livery applied to these vehicles but again showed little sign of PTE ownership in June 1975. / *T. E. Sutch*

Above: This 1967 Roe-bodied Daimler Fleetline is interesting in that the upper deck was rebuilt by Willowbrook in 1974 after an accident. No 4477 still carried Huddersfield colours in October 1974. / *D. Charlton*

Centre left: One of the last vehicles received by Leeds City Transport was this solitary Leyland National. At the time of writing, it remains unique in the West Yorkshire PTE fleet. / *John Fozard*

Bottom left: West Yorkshire PTE instead continued to place Leyland Leopards in service such as 8533, with Plaxton body incorporating dual-purpose seating, seen at Midgley near Halifax in August 1977. / *R. L. Wilson*

Merseyside: Before the PTE

Most of the Merseyside tramway systems were abandoned before the war but Liverpool remained largely dependent on trams until conversion commenced in 1948. The last was replaced in 1957. The motorbus fleet was small until the late 1920s when a considerable number of Karrier and Thornycroft three-axle single-deckers was purchased. Between 1935 and 1940 nearly 200 AEC Regents were added to operate services between suburbs and into new housing estates. The demand for buses in 1940 was so great that 80 elderly Leyland double-deckers were purchased from a dealer.

The disastrous Green Lane depot fire in November 1947 destroyed a large number of tramcars and a fleet of ex-Birmingham Daimler

Liverpool Corporation introduced a City Circle service in December 1965, linking Lime Street, Central and Exchange railway stations with shopping areas. Several Alexander-bodied Leyland PD2/20 Titans were repainted into a livery of cream with green trim and fitted with special destination boards for the service. L161, built in 1955, is shown. / *T. W. Moore*

COG5s was purchased as a stopgap measure. A huge motorbus intake in the 1946-58 period replaced tramcars and old motorbus stock. AEC Regents were purchased throughout but Leyland PD2 Titans took an increasing proportion of the orders. New Daimlers and Crossleys were also received in the late forties. Fleet renewal recommenced in 1962 with distinctively styled Leyland Atlanteans. Immediately before absorption into the PTE, Liverpool had been caught up in the rear-engined single-decker fad but Atlanteans and Bristol VRTs were on order at the time of takeover.

Birkenhead Corporation was highly respected for its fine fleet of buses. Leyland chassis and Massey bodies were normal but by no means exclusive. Batches of Guys and Daimlers were also taken whilst, amongst other bodybuilders, were five Leyland Titans with local Ashcroft bodywork.

Neighbouring Wallasey Corporation also standardised on Leylands but, before the war, manufacturers like Karrier and AEC were also well represented. MCW-bodied Leyland double-deckers dominated postwar purchases, including the first batch of Atlanteans delivered to a municipality. Very few buses were purchased after 1961 so a comparatively elderly fleet was handed over to the PTE. Wallasey Corporation will be remembered by many for its involvement in bus scheduling by computer. It is not surprising that these experiments were not particularly successful when it is realised how little advance has been made in this field as we enter the 1980s.

Southport's early bus fleet included Vulcans but Leylands became standard. Being a popular seaside resort, an open-top fleet has been maintained over the years which has included Bedford OLs, Leyland Titan TD3s succeeded by PD2s, and a trio of ex-Ribble Leyland PS2 Tigers. The one-man fleet operated at the time of takeover in April 1974 included Leyland Panthers, new Atlanteans and, rather unusually, some front-entrance PD2 Titans.

St Helens was alone amongst the municipalities absorbed into Merseyside PTE in being a former trolleybus operator. The tramway system was converted to trolleybus operation between 1927 and 1936. Lowbridge trolleybuses were exclusive to St Helens and the LUT subsidiary, South Lancs Transport, whose trolleybuses were also to be seen in the town. St Helens replaced its trolleybuses between 1952 and 1958, the newer vehicles (of highbridge design) passing to Bradford and South Shields. Leyland motorbuses were popular before the war. Immediately after the war a few Bristols were taken but buses of Leyland and AEC manufacture were usual until takeover by the PTE in April 1974. Notable amongst the AECs were the 40 replicas dating from 1950-2 of London Transport's 'RT' class. Regents and Titans ceased to be purchased after 1967, the fleet then standardising on AEC Swifts.

ight: Liverpool Corporation took elivery of 90 Daimlers in 1949-50, all ut 10 being CVA6 models with AEC 7 litre engines. D519 is seen dwarfing a ubblecar in August 1962 and obviously ad been blessed recently with a repaint though many of this batch of 50 with orthern Counties bodies were off the ad by then. / *G. R. Mills*

Top: Two of the veteran ex-London Transport Leyland Titans that were added to the Liverpool Corporation fleet in the early part of World War II. TD1 24 (KP 3067), nearest the camera, has Short bodywork. / *S. L. Poole*

Above: A newer pair of Liverpool Leylands jostle for position in the City Centre. 1955 Weymann bodied Titan L210, with Liverpool-designed front end, overtakes Metro-Cammell bodied Atlantean L678. The latter is one of the 200 Atlanteans built in 1962-4 to Liverpool specification that breathed new life into bus styling. / *T. W. Moore*

Top: The crew of Liverpool A299 takes a break in June 1953. This was one of the first buses received by Liverpool after the war, being a member of a batch of 100 AEC Regent IIs delivered in 1946-7. The Weymann body was completed by Liverpool Corporation Passenger Transport itself. / *Roy Marshall*

Above: Two more Liverpool Regents. 1954 Mark III (9613S version) A72 overtakes 1957 Mark V (D3RV) A213 in March 1966. Bodies are by Crossley and Metro-Cammell respectively, both being completed by the Corporation. Note the advisory 'Short Journey' destination on A72. / *T. W. Moore*

Right: A Corporation 1929 Leyland Titan TD1, with Leyland body, dominates this splendid period view of buses, trams and costumes at Woodside Ferry, Birkenhead.

Above: Leyland Titans remained popular with Birkenhead Corporation for 40 years. 1938 TD5c 272 carried Northern Counties bodywork. / *Roy Marshall*

Right: This Guy Arab II with Northern Counties body was received by Birkenhead Corporation in 1946. No 354 as seen in September 1948. / *Roy Marshall*

Above right: Satisfactory performance by the wartime Guys led to further batches of Arabs, but with Gardner 6LW engines, being purchased in addition to the usual Titans until 1956. Many received bodies by Birkenhead's favourite coachbuilder, Massey, including 1949 Arab III 149 at Woodside in August 1951. / *Roy Marshall*

Right: Some 1934 deliveries to Wallasey Corporation had Roe centre-entrance bodies, including two of the side-engined AEC Q models. The pair was sold in 1943 to Yeomans Motors, Canon Pyon, near Hereford, an independent operator which collected a number of Q double-deckers from undertakings covered by this book. / *Ian Allan Library*

Left: Wallasey Corporation continued to favour petrol-engined Leyland Titans until 1938. Six TD4c were rebodied by Burlingham in 1949, most unusually retaining the petrol engines and torque converter 'gearless' transmission. Like its five rebodied companions, 105 originally entered service in 1936 with an English Electric body. All six were withdrawn in 1955 and the bodies transferred to new Leyland PD2 chassis. / *S. N. J. White*

PARR 4
Drink Delicious Ty·Phoo TEA as good as good tea can be!
DJ 6864

MAGEE'S ALE
ASHTON 2
306
306
DJ 9184

Above left: 'It's all at the Co-op now' runs today's slogan. No longer available from outside St Helens Co-op, however, is a Corporation trolleybus. No 138 was a Ransomes with Massey bodywork sporting an out-of-character streamline flash in August 1950. / *Roy Marshall*

Left: Only St Helens Corporation and the independent South Lancs Transport ran lowbridge trolleybuses. Corporation 306, a 1943 Sunbeam W/Roe, precedes a veteran SLT Guy in June 1956. / *Roy Marshall*

Above: St Helens Town Hall Square may have changed little but this Corporation 1946 Strachans-bodied Bristol K6A has long been withdrawn. / *Roy Marshall*

Centre right: Southport Corporation owned two of these 1950 Crossley DD42/8 models. The Crossley bodies benefited from straighter lines than was usual from that builder, in harmony with the attractive livery. / *S. E. Letts*

Bottom right: Conductor completes the waybill as passengers alight from Southport Corporation 24, a 1952 Weymann-bodied Leyland Titan PD2/12, unloading in Chapel Street during August 1964. / *Roy Marshall*

Merseyside Passenger Transport Executive

The last open platform double-deckers with Merseyside PTE were those absorbed from St Helens in 1974. Seventeen year old Weymann-bodied Leyland Titan PD2A/30 17 passes St Helens Town Hall in April 1978. / *T. E. Sutch*

It is the writer's view that one of the finest approaches to any city in Britain is the ferry to Liverpool. The Pier Head buildings dominate the skyline, the first introduction to a city that is blessed, despite some suspect suburbs, with a fine centre and a truly unique character.

In addition to the bus and local rail network, the ferries are also the responsibility of the PTE. The opening of the first Mersey road tunnel in July 1934 threatened the ferries but any suggestions of regular bus services through the tunnel were successfully staved off. However it did lead to ideas for a joint board to co-ordinate all forms of transport in the area but these died upon the outbreak of World War II. It was not until after the formation of the PTE that regular bus services

ınder the Mersey finally commenced. Since then ɔublic transport links across the Mersey have urther benefited from the PTE assuming control of ocal rail services.

The two sides of the Mersey are thus being lrawn closer together, contrasting with the ɔosition when the PTE became operational on December 1969. As the buses of the Liverpool livisions were not linked in any way with their :ounterparts south of the Mersey, the PTE riginally adopted two liveries for its buses. .iverpool buses continued the Corporation green ınd cream whilst the blue and primrose of Wirral ɔuses represented the former Birkenhead and Vallasey undertakings. The absorption of St Helens ınd Southport buses in April 1974, painted in lifferent layouts of red and cream, added two more iveries. Buses transferred between divisions had to e completely repainted and eventually a long verdue standard livery of Verona green and ream was introduced throughout the Executive. 'he old mentality still lingers however as Southport pen-toppers, after the odd repaint in standard ivery, are retaining the attractive red and cream ormer Corporation colours. This decision was ollowed by fleetnames and logo in divisional dentifying colours, a subtlety which one suspects is ɔst on the general public!

The PTE's statutory duty under the 1968 Act to ecure or promote an integrated public transport ystem led to an agreement with Crosville and ibble, effective from 30 January 1972. Complete control of the NBC subsidiaries' local services, which suffered from protective fares and restrictions originating from agreements with the former municipal undertakings, was assumed by the PTE to enable integration. The PTE decides service levels and fares, the NBC operators receiving mileage guarantees and reimbursement of costs of operation. The position was modified, of course, by the inclusion of St Helens and Southport from April 1974. The agreement with British Rail was signed in 1973.

PTE bus buying policy has been largely based on the Liverpool favourite, the Leyland Atlantean. The choice of bodybuilders has been rather different, however, with Alexander and East Lancs taking the orders until the Atlantean/MCW combination made a comeback in the late seventies. Earlier PTE Atlanteans were 33ft long with two doors but subsequent deliveries reverted to shorter one-door buses. Other notable deliveries to the PTE include batches of Bristol VRTs with East Lancs bodies (to both the long and short configurations), 50 Daimler Fleetlines with Metro-Cammell bodies and both single- and double-deck versions of the Metro-Scania. An order for a further 110 Fleetlines was cancelled due to delivery delays and Atlanteans and Nationals taken in lieu. Metrobuses and Titans were ordered to evaluate the new generation of double-deckers.

Left: Liverpool Corporation placed a number of largely unpainted vehicles in service. Leyland PD2/30 L308 had its Crossley body completed by Metro-Cammell and took to the road in 1961. Still unpainted after 12 years, L308 could not be described as a pretty sight as it approached Pier Head in August 1973. The BET sticker in the front bulkhead window is not an evocation of the organisation that once owned half the company buses in England and Wales but refers to the Bus Economy Ticket. This was available in Liverpool only and gave a 20% discount on a 10-journey ticket. It could not be used in the Wirral Division, and the introduction of a standardised fare structure following the entry of St Helens and Southport into the PTE led to its withdrawal. / *MRK*

Above right: An interesting vehicle contributed by the Liverpool fleet was this 1956 Leyland Royal Tiger, fitted in 1961 with a 44-seat body by Metro-Cammell for airport services. The raised rear section allowed copious luggage accommodation beneath. XL172 is seen on a private charter in April 1972. / *I. Charlton*

Right: Liverpool Corporation was seduced by the standee single-deck fad which swept the country in the late 1960s. Most of Liverpool's purchases were Leyland Panthers but there were also 25 Bristol RELL6G models with Park Royal bodies, delivered in 1969. Buses like 2024 were a familiar sight on service 1 to Dingle in September 1973. / *M. Fowler*

Below: Typical of ex-Liverpool Leyland Panthers is 1100, with its two-door Metro-Cammell body. This one is on a PTE-inspired rail feeder service in Southport in July 1973, before the latter's municipal bus undertaking became part of the PTE. Merseyside provided the bus and Southport the driver. Standee buses are not popular with British passengers and in most areas double-deckers have returned to favour. The poor reliability of early rear-underfloor-engined single-deckers did not help, for example Merseyside disposed of some of these Panthers after comparatively short lives. / *Roy Marshall*

Above: A number of ex-Birkenhead Leyland Titans passed to other divisions. DBG 131D was transferred to St Helens and painted in the attractive colours of that undertaking. It belonged to the first batch received by Birkenhead to feature the upright front styling adopted by Massey. / *John Fozard*

Left: In company with many ex-Birkenhead Titans, this was one of a number of ex-St Helens AEC Regent V/ Metro-Cammell buses transferred to Liverpool, repainted in the dark green Liverpool colours and numbered in the ex-Liverpool series. Dating from 1962, it was three years newer than the newest ex-Liverpool Regents. A455 approaches Pier Head in October 1974. / *R. L. Wilson*

5
KEW
SUSSEX Rd
LAYCOCK TRAVEL SERVICES
PLEASE PAY DRIVER
BEAVA

2047
30B
WALTON
UKD 541J
HARDY
TO BE LET

Left: Ex-Southport 1965 Leyland PD2/40 53 working in Lord Street in May 1975. Its Weymann body has been made suitable for one-man operation, a relatively unusual conversion for half cab double-deckers. It has since been converted to open-top for summer duties in this seaside town and thus, unlike the rest of the fleet, retains the Southport red and cream colours. / *T. E. Sutch*

Below left: An early delivery to the PTE was this 33ft long Bristol VRT, ordered by Liverpool. The two-door East Lancs body seats 80. / *T. W. Moore*

Top: Two Merseyside PTE Leyland Atlanteans at work near Lime Street station, Liverpool, in August 1973. 1295, built in 1972 with Alexander body, is a 'Cross River Express', its blue and primrose Wirral colours contrasting with the then dark green of the Liverpool fleet. / *MRK*

Above: Also delivered in blue and primrose was Metro-Scania 4002, seen leaving Seacombe Ferry terminus when new in October 1972. / *R. L. Wilson*

Left: Many operators celebrated the Silver Jubilee of Queen Elizabeth II by painting buses in silver livery. A Merseyside example was 1745, a newish East Lancs-bodied Leyland Atlantean, traversing Dale Street, Liverpool, in July 1977. / *R. L. Wilson*

South Yorkshire: Before the PTE

There has always been much to attract the transport enthusiast to this area, not least the three municipal undertakings that combined to form South Yorkshire PTE in April 1974.

Sheffield's much-loved tramway network finally closed in 1960, leaving the town entirely motorbus. The motorbus fleet had been split into three parts since 1929 when a co-ordination agreement with the LMS and LNER meant that a Joint Omnibus Committee took over control of the railway companies' bus services to points outside the City boundary. The 'A' fleet was entirely owned by the Corporation and worked within the City boundary, the 'B' fleet was jointly owned and operated to intermediate points outside the City, whilst the 'C' fleet was completely railway owned and operated

Sheffield Leyland PD2/30 509, with Roe bodywork of teak-aluminium alloy composite construction, entering Fitzalan Square when new in 1958. / *Ian Allan Library*

on longer distance services. British Railways replaced the previous railway companies in 1948, but under the 1968 Transport Act, their interests were transferred to the National Bus Company. On 1 January 1970 the joint committee was dismantled and some buses and longer services passed to NBC subsidiaries.

The Sheffield motorbus fleet has always been varied but vehicles of Leyland and AEC manufacture have generally predominated. This was not necessarily a recipe for standardisation however as a variety of types from each manufacturer was often specified! Daimlers were received during and just after the war but the make did not form an important part of the fleet until the Fleetline era when several batches were taken alongside hundreds of Leyland Atlanteans.

Rotherham Corporation's tramway network had largely been superseded by 1934 except for the joint route to Sheffield via Templeborough, upon which unusual single-ended tramcars were operated until replacement by motorbuses in 1949. Rotherham had introduced trolleybuses in October 1912 and most of the tram conversions of 1929-34 were to the benefit of the 'silent servants'. The fleet became well known for its fast, three-axle centre-entrance single-deck trolleybuses. The extent of trolleybus operation declined somewhat after 1949 but a temporary change of heart led to the rebodying in 1956 of 20 Daimlers with new Roe double-deck bodies. However closure finally took place in October 1965. The motorbus fleet was largely composed of Bristol machines until they ceased to be available to non-nationalised undertakings in the 1950s. Rotherham then went through periods of Crossley, Daimler and AEC buying until commencing standardisation on Fleetlines in 1967.

Doncaster has always been well endowed with independent operators but the Corporation fleet was also of interest. Trams last ran in 1935 but electric traction remained well entrenched in trolleybus form. Roe-bodied Karrier six-wheelers were standard throughout the 1930s although an earlier vehicle was an extremely rare Bristol trolleybus. The liking for three-axle vehicles spread to the motorbus fleet which included several Leyland Titanics and AEC Renowns. Two-axle trolleybuses were received during the war and these were rebodied in the 1950s together with a selection of secondhand trolleybuses which helped replace prewar stock. The last Doncaster trolleybuses ran in 1963 but the modern bodies were not wasted being transferred to Daimler and Leyland motorbus chassis. Before these novelty vehicles, the motorbus fleet was already varied, postwar deliveries having included AECs, Bristols, Daimlers and Leylands. The years immediately preceding the PTE saw the receipt of Daimler Fleetline double-deckers, Seddon single-deckers of varying sizes, and Ford coaches.

Below: The driver clambers in, meaning that passengers bound for Arksey in August 1952 were about to be treated to the sadly missed song of prewar Leylands like Doncaster TS7 No 6. Leyland also built the bodywork — note the sliding door. / *Roy Marshall*

Right: Doncaster 85, a 1943 Guy Arab II with lowbridge Roe body, looked in fine fettle at the Waterdale bus station in May 1952. / *Roy Marshall*

Below: In 1952 Doncaster purchased six of these BUTs with East Lancs bodies, only three years old, from the Darlington system. No 378 is seen on the terminal loop at Bentley in May 1952, showing the non-standard livery initially applied to these vehicles. / *Roy Marshall*

Left: Representing Rotherham Corporation's prewar single-deck trolleybus fleet in this 1935 Guy BT with Craven 32 seat centre-entrance body. / *Ian Allan Library*

Below: A type which did not achieve widespread popularity was the chassisless Bridgemaster, AEC's answer to other builders' lowheight models. Rotherham purchased a few in 1960-1, including 141, carrying the Park Royal bodywork inevitably fitted to production examples. / *T. W. Moore*

Left: The Roe body of Daimler CVG6-30 152 displays the final Rotherham livery style as it approaches Sheffield central bus station in July 1971. / *MRK*

Above left: Rotherham favoured East Lancs-bodied Bristols for many years such as 1950 KS6B 108. The overtaking 1966 AEC Regent V had a shorter career in Rotherham however. Its body is by East Lancs subsidiary, Neepsend. / *T. W. Moore*

Centre left: Blue Ensign was taken over by South Yorkshire PTE in May 1978. The fleet in August 1953 included this 1948 Crossley DD42/7 with bodywork by Scottish Commercial. / *Roy Marshall*

Below: A 1950 Strachans-bodied Leyland PS2 of Sheffield B fleet, seen at Doncaster's Waterdale bus station. / *Don Morris*

Top right: This immaculate 8.8 litre AEC Regal with Chas Roberts body was No 196 in the Sheffield fleet, the railway participation manifesting itself in the fleetname (LMS and LNE Railways) and legal ownership. The picture was taken in September 1934 when the bus was quite new. / *G. H. F. Atkins*

Right: The railway participation enabled Sheffield B and C fleets to specify ECW bodies, then only available to nationalised operators, on five Leyland Leopard L1 chassis in 1961. The resultant splendid combination was unique to Sheffield. No 1182 picks up passengers in Tideswell, Derbyshire, on the Sheffield-Buxton service. / *Leyland Truck & Bus*

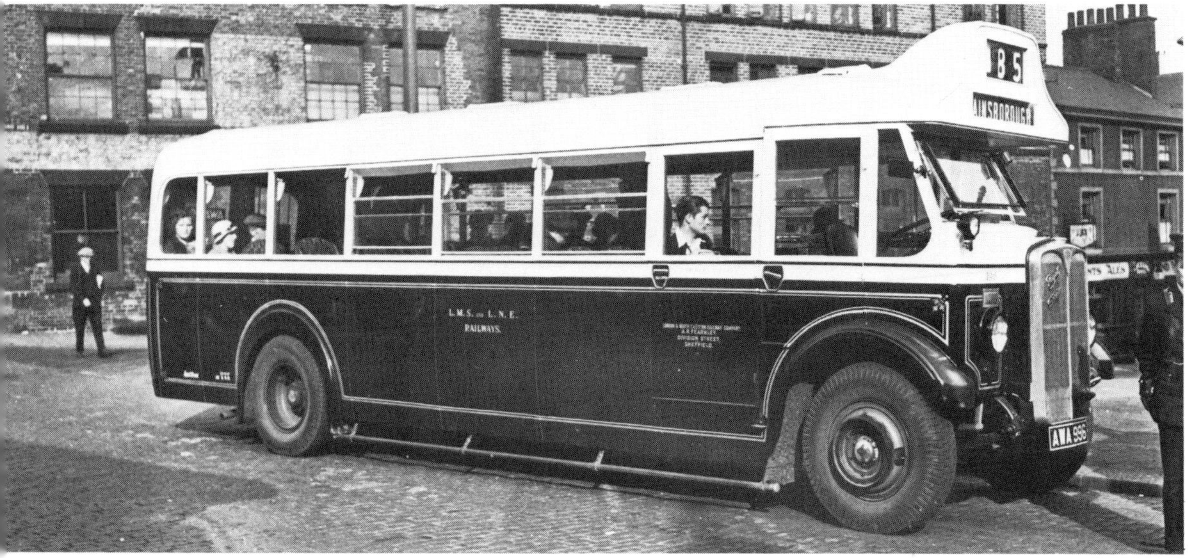
B5
AWA 986

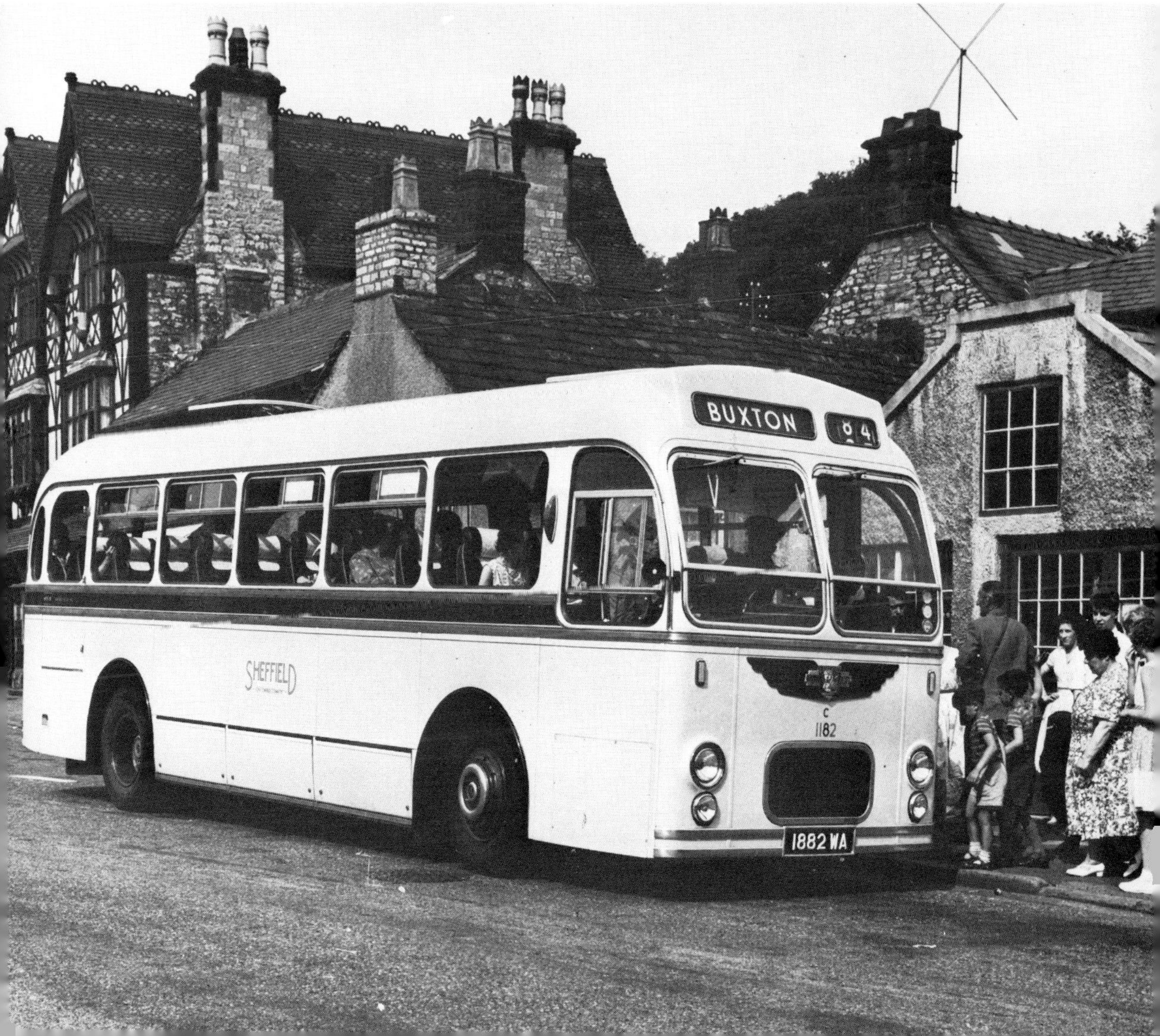
BUXTON
84
SHEFFIELD
C
1182
1882 WA

Above: According to the hoarding, Sheffield United was due to play Birmingham and Middlesbrough at Bramall Lane in September 1929 when Hall Lewis-bodied Karrier 138 (WE 3893), new in 1928, was photographed. / *G. H. F. Atkins*

Centre right: Sheffield painted a number of buses in an all-green livery for a period in the early 1950s. 1938 AEC Regent 395 had just received this new Roe body when seen at Pond Street in July 1952. Note the array of buses in the background. / *Roy Marshall*

Below right: 1942 AEC Regent 466 with rebuilt Massey body passes a remarkable line of fellow wartime deliveries in May 1949. / *Roy Marshall*

Above left: No 45 was the only Sheffield wartime Guy Arab to be rebodied, receiving this Roe body in 1953. It is seen in Bridge Street in June 1954. / *Roy Marshall*

Left: The varied Sheffield fleet had many rarities including No 11, a 1948 Crossley DD42/5 with Northern Coachbuilders body / *Roy Marshall*

Below: More numerous were the Leyland-bodied Leyland Titan PD2s. One of the first, 557, dating from 1947, climbs Barnsley Road, Fir Vale. / *R. F. Mack*

South Yorkshire Passenger Transport Executive

The municipal transport departments of Sheffield, Doncaster and Rotherham were combined on 1 April 1974 to form the South Yorkshire PTE. All three absorbed operators had attractive liveries, the imaginative swoop of the final Doncaster livery was to some extent adopted by West Yorkshire PTE although, of course, the colours were very different. The South Yorkshire PTE choice of a coffee and cream livery in plain style, a marked contrast to what had gone before, received a mixed reception. The brown has since been darkened a couple of shades.

The PTE's early declaration to buy out the remaining independent stage carriage operators within the County further furrowed the brows of local enthusiasts, although no form of compulsory

South Yorkshire PTE National No 2 on Sheffield's City Clipper service in October 1976. / *T. E. Sutch*

urchase is possessed. Booth & Fisher Motor Services of Halfway was taken over in 1976 but etained a measure of independence for some time fterwards. This was followed by the demise of everal Doncaster independents, Felix Motors 1976), Blue Ensign (1978), Blue Line, Reliance and . Severn (1979). One sometimes hears more riticism than praise for the quality of service and olling stock provided by small independent bus perators, but most Doncaster independents were bove reproach in this respect and one mourns the ttractive liveries that have been lost.

South Yorkshire PTE became well known as the nain exponent of a rates-subsidised cheap fares tructure. This is known to check the drift away rom bus travel and is widely favoured on the ontinent as an alternative to expensive and ehumanising road schemes necessitated by ncreased car usage.

The vehicle policy of the PTE has continued the radition of variety favoured by its predecessors. he PTE engineers have experimented in all fields, ncluding battery electric single-deckers. Widely publicised double-deck bus trials were conducted in 1978 when Titan, Metrobus, Ailsa Mark Two, Foden and Dennis Dominator buses were put through their paces on the arduous route 51 (Lodge Moor to Herdings) alongside ordinary PTE Atlanteans and Fleetlines. The order for 120 double-deckers required for 1980 was announced before the end of the trials and comprised equal numbers of Atlanteans and Metrobuses. Experimentation has also embraced different makes of engine and transmission. Most notable however is the introduction of articulated single-deckers on the Sheffield City Clipper service, testing not only the products of three manufacturers (MAN, Volvo and Leyland) but a whole new breed of British bus.

Below: The Leyland articulated buses use expertise from its Danish subsidiary, DAB. Built at the Leyland National factory at Workington, many body parts from the familiar National single-decker are utilised. / *G. K. Gillberry*

Right: Ex-Doncaster Roe-bodied Leyland PD3/4 1177 was nearing the end of 15 years' service in High Street, Doncaster, in June 1977. / *M. Fowler*

Above: West Laithe Gate, Doncaster in May 1978 with Seddon RU 1068 on the Hexthorpe service. The Seddon bodies on this batch originally had two doors but 1068 was rebuilt to single entrance/exit and had a longer life than its fellows. / *M. Fowler*

Left: Ex-Rotherham 1968 Daimler Fleetline/Roe No 1488 climbs away from the bus station in April 1977. / *M. Fowler*

Left: Several of these ex-Doncaster 1965 Leyland Royal Tiger Cubs were transferred to Booth & Fisher operations. No 1038 is seen at the Halfway garage in June 1978 displaying a rather surprising destination for a South Yorkshire service! (This Wales is east of Sheffield). The Royal Tiger Cub was a heavier duty version of the Leopard, and the 20 taken by Doncaster were the only home market examples. The Roe bodies were 33ft 6in long. / *M. Fowler*

Below: Booth & Fisher Roe-bodied AEC Reliance 864 KNU, with faded destination blind, seen at Thorpe Salvin on the Worksop-Beighton service in August 1975. / *M. Fowler*

Left: Sheffield received 18 of these East Lancs-bodied Bristol VRTs in 1972. They replaced an order for 25 Bristol RE saloons and underlined the return to favour of the double-decker. No 279, working from Doncaster, awaits custom at the 175 terminus in Sandringham Road, Intake, in October 1977. This was a permanent transfer, but loans from Sheffield are also usually used on service 175 because, there being an Intake in Sheffield, buses can show a destination without receiving Doncaster blinds. / *M. Fowler*

Right: The Alexander body of this 1973 Leyland AN68 is fitted with a special camera for vandal surveillance, a sad reflection on present-day society. 289 leaves Doncaster (southern bus station) in May 1978. / *M. Fowler*

Left: Before adopting the style shown above, Alexander supplied some bodies of this design to Sheffield. 1972 Daimler Fleetlines 251 and 261, still in full Sheffield livery including fleetname, await their next spell of work from Sheffield's central bus station in August 1977. / *MRK*

Right: The attempt to update Eastern Coach Works standard double-deck body into the modern idiom resulted in a fleet of 56 Daimler Fleetlines of this appearance, delivered to South Yorkshire in 1974-5. Note the small corner windows added to eliminate blind spots from the cab. Central bus station, Sheffield, August 1977. / *MRK*

Three pictures taken on Doncaster's Inner Circle service.
Above and centre: South Yorkshire's interest in electric buses is exemplified by these two vehicles working the service on 1 August 1977. No 1000, one of two 1972 Willowbrook-bodied Crompton 'Electricar's' bought from the Department of the Environment in 1976, hums along Church Way near the Northern bus station. Meanwhile Greater Manchester PTE's 1975 Seddon/Lucas battery electric bus loads at Christ Church. / *M. Fowler*

Below: The Inner Circle is usually operated by Seddon Midis but in September 1977 ex-Felix AEC Reliance/Roe 1012 was helping out. It wore its 17 years lightly as seen in this view at Christ Church. / *M. Fowler*

Right: Only four Metro-Scania Metropolitans were taken into the South Yorkshire PTE fleet. No 502 is seen when new at Doncaster in May 1975. Note the County Council coat of arms which was only used for a short period. / *M. Fowler*

Below: The PTE ordered 62 Volvo Ailsas to be fitted with Alexander bodies. However the body order was changed to the benefit of Van Hool McArdle resulting in a combination that is not now likely to be repeated. No 389 demonstrates the distinctive lines as it leaves Doncaster's southern bus station in October 1976, the year the buses were built. / *T. E. Sutch*

Left: A batch of Daimler Fleetlines received by South Yorkshire PTE had MCW bodies to London Transport DM style. No 1502 is seen in Sheffield's Central bus station on its first day in service in March 1977. / *J. Armytage*

Right: This East Lancs bodied Dennis Dominator, numbered 522 in the South Yorkshire fleet, was used as a demonstrator by Hestair Dennis carrying PTE style livery but with light blue instead of brown relief. It is seen working for the PTE in Abbey Lane, Sheffield in March 1978. / *J. Armytage*

Left: There is little to distinguish the solitary Foden in the fleet. East Lancs-bodied 511 stands at Sheffield Lane Top in March 1978. / *J. Armytage*

Tyne and Wear: Before the PTE

Two passengers alight from a Newcastle Corporation 1935 Karrier E4A via the front exit. No 40 (CVK 52) is typical of Newcastle's first generation of trolleybuses built between 1935 and 1940. Nearly all carried similar Metro-Cammell 60-seat twin-door, twin-staircase bodywork and were based on Karrier, AEC or Guy chassis. The prewar fleet was replaced by new stock in 1949-50. This view is thought to have been taken in January 1939. / *Ian Allan Library*

Newcastle Corporation introduced motorbuses before World War I but bus services really got under way in the 1920s. At first they were viewed as an extension of the Corporation's large tramway network and included services of a distinctly rural nature. Some of the latter passed to United Automobile Services in the 1930s, together with some single-deck buses, allowing the Corporation to concentrate on city and suburban routes.

The motorbuses were painted blue and the network was marketed as 'Blue Bus Services', this title dwarfing that of Newcastle Corporation Transport on literature. AEC buses became established in the 1920s, followed by the products of ADC (the short-lived partnership between AEC and Daimler). For a time after the dissolution of that

partnership, vehicles from both manufacturers captured most of the orders but Daimlers were standard from 1933 until World War II. A few of the Daimlers were of lowbridge specification for the Ponteland and Darras Hall services, and a small number of postwar double-deckers was of similar specification.

Trolleybuses were introduced to supersede tramcars in Newcastle from 1935. By the outbreak of war an impressive fleet of yellow-painted three-axle trolleybuses was in service, of AEC, Guy and Karrier manufacture. A feature was the separate front exit. Petrol and diesel fuel shortages during the wartime years laid greater strain on the trolleybus and tramcar networks. Trolleybuses were hired from Bournemouth and Brighton Corporations whilst 10 English Electric vehicles (older than the Newcastle system itself) were purchased from Bradford. Eighteen wartime Karrier vehicles, the first Newcastle two-axle trolleybuses, enabled the conversion of the Elswick Road route in 1944 — tram to trolley conversions were, by necessity, rare in the wartime years.

Tram replacement was completed in the early postwar years using both trolleybuses and buses — buses adopting the yellow trolleybus livery in 1949. The trolleybus fleet was re-equipped with two and three-axle vehicles of Sunbeam and BUT manufacture, their Northern Coachbuilders and Metro-Cammell bodies lacking the separate front exit of the prewar fleet. Daimlers again featured in the earliest postwar motorbus deliveries but AEC Regents and Leyland Titans dominated the orders until the Leyland Atlantean became standard from 1960. The trolleybuses were superseded by motorbuses between 1963 and 1966.

The first motorbus services under the aegis of Sunderland Corporation were not introduced until 1928 and involved hired buses and crews from Northern General. The hired vehicles were replaced by Leyland Lions in 1929. Double-deck buses (of Dennis manufacture) first appeared in 1930.

The motorbuses posed a threat to the Sunderland tramway network but the new manager appointed in 1929, Charles Hopkins, instead recommended modernisation of the system. The tramcar fleet became a great source of interest to enthusiasts and the distinctive approach to tramway operation was reflected in the motorbus fleet, which standardised on centre-entrance Daimlers between 1934 and the outbreak of war. One-man operated single-deckers were introduced in 1939. A large number of austerity specification Guys was received during the war years, some of which were rebodied by Roe in 1954-5.

The pro-tram policy finally ended in 1946 with a decision to phase them out, this being achieved between 1950 and 1954. The motorbus livery changed from red and cream to green and cream in 1952. Early postwar buses were generally of Daimler and Guy manufacture although, like prewar, a small number of Crossleys was included. There were also some Atkinson and AEC saloons. The first Daimler Fleetlines broke new ground in double-deck body design in 1962. In 1966, Sunderland Corporation boldly decided to introduce a flat-fare (later zonal fare) token system using omo saloons. A large fleet of distinctively-styled rear-engined single-deckers was rapidly built up based on AEC, Bristol, Daimler and Leyland chassis.

South Shields' first buses were Edison battery electric vehicles, introduced in 1914. Ordinary petrol buses appeared in 1919. Daimler single-deckers purchased in 1934 were the beginning of the undertaking's preference for Gardner-powered diesel buses. The bus fleet was still very small at this time, numbering only 10 vehicles.

Trolleybuses were introduced in 1936, and were of Karrier manufacture. The Weymann bodies in their blue and yellow livery bore more than a passing resemblance to Bradford vehicles. The red and cream livery on the existing motorbus fleet changed to the 'Bradford' colours too but the specification of front entrances on South Shields' immediate prewar Daimlers was not then shared by the Yorkshire town. The last South Shields tramcar ran in 1946.

Karrier and Sunbeam trolleybuses were received after the war including some secondhand examples from the Pontypridd and St Helens networks. Trolleybuses were, however, phased out between 1958 and 1964.

Crossley motorbuses were taken into stock in the earliest postwar years but Guys were standard throughout the 1950s. Control of Guys passed to Daimler and the short-length Guy Arab chassis favoured by South Shields temporarily ceased to be available. Front-engined Daimlers were thus specified from 1960, switching to Fleetlines in 1965. Single-deck one-man-operated buses were introduced from 1967 in the form of two batches of Bristol RESLs. Six single-deck Fleetlines were on order at the time of absorption into Tyneside PTE.

Above: Newcastle Corporation's first four AEC Regents, delivered in January 1930, may have heralded the modern generation but is was still necessary to start the engine on the handle. Nos 99-102 had open-staircase Hall Lewis bodywork but, by the time a subsequent batch (with enclosed staircases) was delivered, the bodybuilders had changed their name to something more familiar nowadays — Park Royal. A scene at Haymarket, most probably in 1930. / *AEC*

Right: Uncompromisingly angular even after a refit, Newcastle Corporation 'Blue Bus' 248 was a 1943 Guy Arab I with Strachans lowbridge body. September 1947. / *R. A. Mills*

Above left: This Newcastle Corporation Daimler CWA6 had an interesting history. Delivered just after the war, it was first fitted with a 1932 Metro-Cammell body originally on a petrol-engined AEC Regent. Even Metro-Cammell bodies eventually wear out, however, and in 1950 the Daimler was given this new, rare, Mann Egerton body. The bus also had the distinction of being numbered 1 in the fleet, as seen here near Central station. / *R. F. Mack*

Left: Amongst the first Newcastle Corporation motorbuses to appear in the yellow livery were 40 AEC Regent IIIs, with 'ECW look' Northern Coachbuilders bodies in 1950. One of the batch, 322, overtakes a veteran Scammell Scarab of British Railways. Another, 341, is now privately preserved and, like 123, occasionally operates on special services. / *C. Carter*

ight: Newcastle's all-Leyland PD2 itans had long lives but two are seen ere in their original blue livery. One of iese 1948 examples, 123, is now the roperty of Tyne and Wear County ouncil Museums. It was been restored to iis livery and occasionally operates on becial services. / *Ian Allan Library*

Above right: This well-proportioned style of Northern Coachbuilders body went to a number of operators on both bus and trolleybus chassis. Newcastle Corporation 500 was a 1948 Sunbeam S7 and the 70-seat body was a local product, the NCB factory being in Claremont Road, Spital Tongues. / *R. L. Wilson*

Right: No 583 passes Monument in April 1966, six months before final trolleybus closure. By this time the only trolleybuses remaining were these 1950 BUT 9641Ts with Metro-Cammell 70-seat bodies. The design of this batch was based on 20 earlier Newcastle trolleybuses, a diverted London Transport order, hence the 'Q1' look about 583. / *Ian Allan Library*

Below: January weather in Newcastle is not conducive to spotless buses. A 1956 Park Royal-bodied AEC Regent V of the synchromesh gearbox MD3RV variety demonstrates the effectiveness of the salting and gritting crews in 1969. / *T. W. Moore*

Left: Fog on the Tyne. A murky day in South Shields as 202, one of the series of Weymann-bodied Karrier E4s supplied to the Corporation in 1936-7, prepares to make a journey to Marsden in April 1952. */ Roy Marshall*

Above: Early postwar Karrier W/ Northern Coachbuilders 252 enjoys considerably better weather as it speeds through Tyne Dock in September 1963. The position of the bamboo trolley retrieval pole above the lower saloon windows is typically South Shields. */ A. Moyes*

Left: Corporation 1948 Roe-bodied Crossley DD42/5 No 143 stands in South Shields Market Place in June 1954, long before the area was rebuilt. */ Roy Marshall*

Top left: Sunderland Corporation pioneered one-man operation long before it became a financial necessity with urban operators. This Crossley Mancunian II with 32-seat Blagg body was an extremely unusual purchase in 1939. / *Don Morris*

Centre left: Quite possibly the only centre-entrance wartime Guy Arab was Sunderland 59, a 1942 Mark I with Roe body of the style fitted to the Corporation's prewar Daimlers. It is seen in September 1947. / *R. A. Mills*

Below: Another 1942 Guy Arab I in the Sunderland fleet was ABV 867 which was acquired from Blackburn Corporation in 1947. It was numbered 6 in both fleets and carried a Pickering body. No 6 wore red livery when seen in John Street, Sunderland, in June 1954. / *Roy Marshall*

Right: Also seen in June 1954 was No 20, a 1946 Crossley DD42/3 with Craven body, in Sunderland's then new green livery. / *Roy Marshall*

Below right: The Anderson and Wilson partnership trading as 'The Economic Bus Service' was taken over by Tyne and Wear on 1 January 1975. Wilson at one time owned this 1945 Albion CX13 with Pickering body seen in Sunderland during June 1954. / *Roy Marshall*

SHOP AT BINNS
SCT
DOCKS
Have a CAPSTAN — made to make friends
GR 8251

PARK LANE CAFE
QUICK SNACKS
Pepsi-Cola
ECONOMIC
O. SHIELDS
ECONOMIC
DUPLICATE
Economic

Tyne and Wear Passenger Transport Executive

An area scheme for the north-east was proposed following the 1947 Transport Act, but generated little enthusiasm amongst operators likely to be involved. There was thus no change until 1 January 1970, when the Newcastle and South Shields municipal transport departments were transferred to the new Tyneside Passenger Transport Executive. The two centres of operation were not linked by bus services acquired by the new PTE, interurban routes in the area being provided by the Northern group of companies (by this time part of the NBC).

Newcastle was very much the senior contributor, handing over a large fleet of Leyland Atlanteans to the Executive. A few Leyland Panthers and some surviving AEC Regents and

The Scania-engined Metropolitan found considerable favour with Tyne & Wear PTE. 1976 example No 739 is seen in Percy Street, Newcastle, in July 1978 followed by a Northern group Leyland Atlantean in PTE-inspired yellow livery. / *MRK*

Leyland Titans also passed to the PTE. The South Shields fleet still contained a good proportion of rear-entrance Guys and Daimlers, supplemented by modern Fleetlines and Bristol REs.

On 1 April 1974, the Tyne and Wear Metropolitan County came into being. The new body assumed control of the PTE which became responsible for all public transport within the County including, amongst other areas, Sunderland. The name was accordingly changed to the Tyne and Wear Passenger Transport Executive. In anticipation of these changes, Sunderland Corporation had transferred its transport undertaking to Tyneside PTE with effect from 1 April 1973.

Again there was no operational link between Sunderland and the rest of the PTE. The Sunderland fleet at this time mostly consisted of Daimler Fleetline double-deckers and the rear-engined single-deck stock which had revolutionised the undertaking in the late 1960s. A few rear platform buses also still survived.

In August 1973 the related companies of R. Armstrong (Bus Proprietor) Ltd, a delightful name, and Galley's Coaches Ltd were acquired by the PTE. Galley's had been acquired by Armstrong in 1961. A fleet of Bedford and AEC coaches was thus taken into stock whilst Armstrong also contributed four secondhand double-deckers — three AEC Regent Vs and an ex-London Transport RTL. This purchase gave the PTE a firm base on which to develop its coaching interests. The old-established names have been retained on the current coach fleet which carry PTE livery and symbol.

On 1 January 1975, a PTE link was at last forged between Sunderland and South Shields. This was the high-frequency service between the two towns acquired with the partnership of Anderson and Wilson of Whitburn, trading as 'The Economic Bus Service'. Bedfords and AECs were again added to stock. Although a similar link remains unfulfilled between Newcastle and South Shields, the PTE has an agreement with both NBC companies in its area (Northern and United) whereby the PTE specifies the pattern and levels of service, and the fares charged (subject to the approval of the Traffic Commissioners, of course). Northern in fact paints certain of its buses operating within Tyne & Wear in yellow and white although the layout of the colours is to NBC standard.

The PTE has increasingly tended towards a short-life vehicle policy. Leyland Atlanteans with single- or double-door bodywork are now in service in all three centres of operation. Volvo Ailsas purchased in 1975 failed to attract further orders but since that date the Atlantean double-deck monopoly has been severely dented by deliveries of Metropolitans and Fleetlines.

Other PTE responsibilities include the North Shields-South Shields ferry. Of the local rail services, the North Tyne Loop and the Newcastle-South Shields branch will form part of the much-heralded electric Metro rapid transit system. In providing a fully integrated bus and rail network, the Metro is bound to have a profound effect on bus services and will include four major transport interchanges. Closure of part of the North Tyneside rail service for conversion to Metro led to the introduction of special Rail Link express bus services using older PTE stock, the interesting feature being their operation in some cases by United driving staff.

Left: Alexander-bodied Leyland Atlantean 101 was transferred to the Armstrong's subsidiary of the PTE but is seen here assisting on ordinary services. It started life in 1963 with Newcastle Corporation and, like the Daimler on page 95, was No 1 in that fleet. / *John Fozard*

Below: The body contracts for Newcastle's Leyland Atlanteans were split between the MCW group and Alexander, the former successfully modifying its standard shell to resemble that of the latter. Compare Metro-Cammell-bodied 211, built in 1966 and seen in September 1977, with 101 above. / *M. Fowler*

Below: A batch of these 36ft long Daimler Fleetline single-deckers with Marshall bodies was ordered by South Shields but delivered to Tyneside PTE in 1971. No 356 is seen in South Shields Market Place that year. It was renumbered more than once, an eventual fleet number 1986 being one of the highest used by Tyne and Wear. / *Roy Marshall*

Above: Sunderland's first Daimler Fleetlines were an early attempt to get away from the box shape of rear-engined double-deckers, hence the peak and cutaway rear end of Roe-bodied 263 seen with Tyne and Wear in September 1974. / *Roy Marshall*

Left: Sunderland Corporation went into one-man operation in a big way by largely re-equipping its fleet with standee single-deckers. Typical is this 1968 Leyland Panther swinging into Olive Street, Sunderland, in July 1978 as Tyne and Wear 1931. The sloping pillars of the Strachans body are typically Sunderland. / *MRK*

Below left: Sunderland collected a number of former Edinburgh Guys and Leylands for use as driver training buses. LFS 410 was eventually repainted in the Newcastle-inspired PTE livery and, being a 1954 Metro-Cammell 'Orion'-bodied Leyland PD2, had more than a superficial resemblance to Newcastle's first lightweight Leylands, 351-3. The bus had acquired fleet 'number' DT6 by April 1977. / *M. Fowler*

Above: A 1972 Leyland Panther with Alexander dual-purpose body seen a year later near Newcastle University. Note the Tyneside PTE fleetname on the front dash. / *Roy Marshall*

Right: Six of the former Standerwick Bristol VRLLH6L motorway coaches that did not find favour with National Travel (North West) passed to Tyne and Wear in 1976 for the Tyne Commission Quay passenger transfer service to and from Newcastle Central station. No 33 was still only six years old when seen at Newcastle Central station in July 1978. The PTE favoured this livery with its greater area of cream for a short period before adopting the present very attractive yellow and white. / *MRK*

Below right: Ten of the first Volvo Ailsas were supplied to various PTEs in 1974-5. Tyne and Wear took three but ordered no more. The trio was initially operated in Newcastle but subsequently was transferred to Sunderland. No 412, with sleek Alexander bodywork, turns into Olive Street in July 1978. All three were withdrawn from service soon after. / *MRK*

Left: Large numbers of Atlanteans and Fleetlines with Alexander bodywork of this general appearance have been supplied to Tyne and Wear. Fleetline No 820 is well laden as it turns into Holmeside, Sunderland, in July 1978. The standard PTE destination display deserves full marks for clarity. / *MRK*

Right: The small windows of the 30 Willowbrook-bodied Leyland Atlanteans received in 1977-8 contrast with the panoramic Alexander bodies. No 583 shows the nearside staircase favoured by the PTE for many of its buses. The scene is again Holmeside, Sunderland, in July 1978. / *MRK*

Below: The PTE has re-equipped the Armstrong Galley coaching fleet. The 1977 Bedford YMT with 53-seat Plaxton coachwork awaits a party in Newcastle in July 1978. / *MRK*

The West Midlands: Before the PTE

The largest contributor to the West Midlands PTE was Birmingham City Transport which, at one time, operated 1,800 buses. Birmingham was held in high regard throughout the industry, attention to detail manifesting itself in a fleet of well designed and scrupulously maintained buses, painted in a dignified dark blue and cream.

Daimlers and Tilling-Stevens were chosen in the earliest days but AECs had gained favour by the time big orders began to be placed in the mid-1920s. Diesel buses saw the re-introduction of Daimlers, their initial appeal being their 'easychange' preselective gearboxes and economical Gardner engines. Daimler was to dominate orders right up to PTE days. Leyland established itself as an alternative supplier

A Coventry Transport 1936 Brush-bodied Daimler COA6, seen just after the war in Earl Street. / *T. W. Moore Collection*

however between 1938 and 1949 whilst Crossley completed orders for 270 buses in 1949-50 to assist in the tramway replacement and fleet renewal programmes. Guys then took over as alternative supplier between 1950 and 1954, providing large numbers of 'Arabs' with preselective gearboxes. By the end of 1954, the fleet was almost entirely of postwar construction. Virtually no changes were thus made until the earliest postwar buses fell due for replacement in 1961. After comparative trials between Leyland Atlanteans and Daimler Fleetlines, large orders were placed for the latter. To avoid a repeat of the seven-year lull, fleet replacement was taken at a more leisurely pace which meant that by takeover in 1969 some buses had already approached 20 years' service — no problem thanks to their sturdy design.

Mention must also be made of the relatively small Birmingham trolleybus network, these vehicles being operated on the Nechells service between 1922 and 1940, and on the Coventry Road group between 1934 and 1951.

The next largest contributor was Midland 'Red'. It too operated Tilling-Stevens buses in the early days, some of which passed to Birmingham Corporation in 1914 with the 'Red' services entirely within Birmingham (reminiscent of the 1973 takeover by the PTE of Midland 'Red' services entirely within the West Midlands area). From 1923 Midland 'Red' was unusual in manufacturing its own buses, until 1940 under the initials SOS and then, on resumption after the war, the initials BMMO. The wartime years saw buses of outside manufacture enter the fleet and further buses from AEC, Guy and Leyland were added when double-deckers were urgently needed after the war. Production of BMMO buses slowed in the 1960s and batches of Leyland Leopards and Daimler Fleetlines assisted until BMMO production ceased in 1970. At the time of the 1973 takeover, Midland 'Red' was pursuing a single-deck only policy, standardising on Nationals. An interesting comparison is that early post-war fleet renewal was much slower than BCT, large scale rebuilding enabling pre-war stock to last until the late 1950s. This meant that throughout the 1950s, Midland 'Red' had many more veterans on its books than BCT. However in the 1960s the position was reversed with BCT finding itself with an increasingly ageing fleet whilst the 'Red' moved towards a target vehicle life of 12 years.

The products of Guy Motors naturally found favour in their home town of Wolverhampton, from the massive six-wheelers of the twenties to the relatively rare semi-automatic gearbox Arabs of the 1960s. Daimlers also featured in orders between 1934 and 1950. Wolverhampton Corporation was an enthusiastic early user of the trolleybus, putting large numbers into service in the 1920s. The extensive network was replaced in favour of motorbuses in the 1960s, the last trolleybuses operating in 1967. Motorbus renewal was interrupted whilst the trolleybus replacement programme proceeded, meaning that the oldest members of the Wolverhampton fleet became the oldest motorbuses in the new undertaking.

Walsall was an enthusiastic user of Dennis buses before the war, but the performance of the Guy 'austerity' buses allocated in 1942-5 evidently impressed as allegiance switched to Guys until 1951. The fleet then seemed set for a 'Leyland period' but the standardisation of the past was shattered by the appointment of Mr R. Edgley Cox as General Manager. Buses of several makes were added and variety was increased by the lengthening of a few older vehicles. This step was followed by several orders for specially shortened Daimler Fleetlines, but culminating in an order for a solitary giant 36ft long Daimler double-decker!

Trolleybuses had been introduced in 1931 and this network was developed by Mr Edgley Cox. Lengthening occurred in the trolleybus fleet too but there were also several notable batches of secondhand vehicles to add to the variety. Apart from the loss of the jointly operated Walsall-Wolverhampton service, the entire network was intact in 1969.

The vehicle policies of West Bromwich and Coventry Corporations were quite similar after very different starts. West Bromwich initially favoured the products of Guy and Dennis whilst Coventry took Maudslays. Both switched to Daimlers in the 1930s, often with Metro-Cammell bodies. Both rebuilt or rebodied their wartime intake. The introduction of Daimler Fleetlines saw both operators turning to bodybuilders new to them. The Coventry fleet will, however, be remembered for its preference for AEC-engined Daimlers, standard between 1934 and 1950, and exclusive to that town in prewar years.

Right: Birmingham City Transport had 50 AEC Regents dating from 1929-31 rebodied by Brush during the war to extend their lives. No 402 is seen on driving tuition work. / *A. Yates*

Above: The 800 Daimler COG5 buses delivered to BCT between 1934 and 1940 included 35 single-deckers. This prewar scene shows 1935 model 43, with Metro-Cammell 34-seat body, at what is now known as the Queen Elizabeth Hospital. / *G. B. Sampson*

Right: The body style associated with Birmingham's COG5 double-deckers was also to be found in trolleybus form. 1937 Leyland TB5/Metro-Cammell No 76 prepares to turn right into Carrs Lane from the Bull Ring, long before the latter's reconstruction. / *C. Carter*

Left: The extensive fleet renewal programme adopted by BCT just after the war meant the simultaneous withdrawal of several different types of bus. Seen awaiting sale in 1950 are 1939 Leyland Titan TD6c No 275, 1937 Daimler COG5 1064, both with Metro-Cammell bodies, and 1944 Guy Arab II/Park Royal 1407. / *R. A. Mills*

Below: Part of the new fleet was this Daimler CVG6 with Metro-Cammell body, typical of its generation of solid and reliable buses. No 1592 entered service on the first day of 1948 and looks as good as new in Paradise Street during May 1963. / *D. Kirk*

Right: Non-standard buses bought by Birmingham City Transport to speed fleet renewal included 50 of these Park Royal-bodied Leyland PD2 Titans, delivered in 1949-50. No 2217 traverses Paradise Street in June 1968 on one of the services that were technically jointly operated with Midland Red — hence the 'B' prefix to the service number, denoting a Midland Red Birmingham local service. / *MRK*

Below: Inspector has a word with the driver of No 2255, assisting on the normally double-decked 61 service. No 2255 is one of 30 Leyland PS2 Tigers which, with five Leyland Olympics, took over from the COG5 single-deckers in 1950. Despite their old-fashioned specification, the Tigers had long lives, 2255 being photographed in Navigation Street in April 1969. / *MRK*

Right: Some of the 260 Crossleys delivered to Birmingham City Transport within only 12 months in 1949-50 bridged the gap between the traditional BCT bus and the 'new look' vehicles to follow, combining the exposed radiator and earlier destination layout with sliding ventilators. A small boy acts suspiciously as No 2392 thunders into Melvina Road from Saltley Road in June 1967. / *Paul Gray*

Left: Two Crossley-bodied Daimler CVG6s swapped their 'Birmingham' front ends (see page 122) for 'Manchester' fronts — so-called because the glassfibre assembly was first supplied to that operator. 'Manchester' front No 2880 loads at Cotteridge in March 1969. / *MRK*

Below: Ten of the 1964 Daimler Fleetlines incorporated two new designs of windscreen. No 3393 was one of six with V-screens which were subsequently adopted as standard. It is seen passing the Halfords premises in Lancaster Place during January 1965. These buildings are now the headquarters of the West Midlands County Council, still known facetiously to some as 'the bike warehouse', in memory of the previous tenants. Today the scene is dominated by a flyover and appropriately named Lancaster Circus. / *T. W. Moore*

Left: Coventry Transport received a large number of austerity buses following the devastation of the town, and its bus and tram fleet, in the early part of World War II. This 1943 Guy Arab II lasted until 1958, the angular lines of its Weymann body changing little despite rebuilding by the Corporation. / *T. W. Moore*

Below: An unusual purchase for a municipal operator was this Bedford SB5 with Duple coachwork, added to the Coventry fleet in 1964. No 404 is seen leaving Harnall Lane garage when new. / *T. W. Moore*

Right: West Bromwich High Street was well endowed with Corporation buses in April 1953. Two of the Daimler CVG6/ Weymanns received the previous year lead the procession but the second is challenged by No 91, a 1939 Metro-Cammell-bodied Daimler COG6. / *Ian Allan Library*

Below right: The next batch of West Bromwich buses, Daimler CVG6s with Metro-Cammell bodies delivered in 1955, had 'new look' fronts. No 183 clearly shows the ornate livery of two shades of blue with cream, relieved by gold and black lining. / *Ian Allan Library*

CHEMISTS
TIMOTHY WHITES & TAYLORS
BIRMINGHAM
WEDNESBURY
VIA WEST BROMWICH
75
10
74
GEA 173

BIRMINGHAM
DUDLEY
VIA WEST BROMWICH
74
Cammies and Cadman
HAIR STYLISTS
HOOPER BROS LTD
KEA 183

Right: Many of Walsall Corporation's wartime Guys received Park Royal bodies from the prewar fleet of Dennis Lance buses. The prewar bodies had lasted better than the wartime ones, which were built at a time when good timber was unobtainable. No 51 is about to be overtaken in Walsall bus station by a 1951 Leyland PD2/Park Royal with full width cab. / *Roy Marshall*

Right: Other wartime deliveries to Walsall Corporation included Sunbeam W trolleybuses, like No 324 with Brush body. / *Roy Marshall*

Right: Initial post-war deliveries to Walsall Corporation were Park Royal-bodied Guy Arabs. No 254, with somewhat rebuilt body, awaits departure from the busy bus station in March 1963. / *M. C. Beamish*

Above: The 22 Sunbeam F4A trolleybuses delivered to Walsall in 1954-6 were notable because they were 30ft long, longer than was then permitted for two-axle double-deckers, and were operated under special dispensation from the Ministry of Transport. The composite construction bodies by Willowbrook seated 70. No 860 at Bloxwich.
/ *Ian Allan Library*

Left: The Corporations of Walsall and Wolverhampton ran a jointly operated trolleybus service between the two towns. Seen outside Cleveland Road garage during the war is Wolverhampton No 270, a 1938 Sunbeam MF2 with Park Royal body.
/ *West Midlands PTE archives*

Left: Guys naturally predominated in the fleet of their home town, Wolverhampton. 1953 Roe-bodied Arab IV No 571 stands below St Peters in Wulfruna Street. Like their companions in Birmingham, these were rare amongst home market Guys in possessing pre-selector rather than 'crash' gearboxes. / *Ian Allan Library*

Below: The subsequent 30ft long Arab IVs and Vs had semi-automatic gearboxes, also fairly rare. Churchyard trees provide the background to Arab IV No 20 as it awaits departure time from the village of Pattingham in 1959. / *Ian Allan Library*

Top: Guy did not win all the Wolverhampton orders. These three S.M.C. (Sunbeam) Pathan buses were added in 1930, with bodies by Herbert E. Taylor & Co Ltd, Eaton Coachworks, Norwich. They were intended for the longer distance routes from Wolverhampton such as to Bridgnorth and Cannock, both since handed over to Midland Red. / *Ian Allan Library*

Above: Ten AEC-engined Guy Arabs delivered in 1963 were followed in 1966 by five AEC Renowns. The Nottingham-style bodies were truly MCW group productions, being commenced by Weymann and completed by Metro-Cammell. No 184 loads in Exchange Street in July 1966. / *T. W. Moore*

Right: Midland Red 1932 SOS DD(RE) HA 8038 at Pool Meadow, Coventry, in 1935, ready for the sprint to Birmingham. / *A. J. Owen*

Below: Midland Red SOS SON 1923, built in 1936, received a non-standard cab after an accident, but the rest of the English Electric body had also been extensively rebuilt by the time it was photographed working the erstwhile 183 route in Shirley. / *G. H. Stone*

Right: The early post-war Midland Red buses were years ahead of their time, the underfloor-engined single-deckers being based on wartime prototypes. This BMMO S9 type, 3400, was built in 1949 and is seen in Dudley bus station. / *A. D. Broughall*

Below: Two views of the bus park at Dudley bus station, before and after takeover by West Midlands PTE. The upper view shows Midland Red buses in 1964, including S17, D9, LD8, D7 and S16 classes. The lower view, in 1975, shows S17, S23 and D9 types. The khaki roof specimens just visible in the background are CVG6 Daimlers ex-West Bromwich and Birmingham. The latter would be on loan to an ex-Midland Red garage. / *T. W. Moore*

West Midlands Passenger Transport Executive

The PTE came into being on 1 October 1969, absorbing on that date the municipal transport departments of Birmingham, Walsall, West Bromwich and Wolverhampton. The first three had favoured various shades of blue so the choice of a Birmingham-style livery with a large area of cream accompanied by a brighter shade of blue was not surprising.

Birmingham contributed almost equal numbers of front and rear-engined buses to the PTE. The former consisted almost entirely of Daimlers and Guys dating from 1950-4 whilst the latter were almost entirely Daimler Fleetlines. The relatively small single-deck fleet included Fords, AEC Swifts and more Fleetlines, but a handful of Leyland Tigers was a reminder of an earlier era.

Disused trolleybus wires remain in position as replacement buses work the newly converted routes out of Walsall bus station in October 1970. New Daimler Fleetline/Northern Counties No 4015, ordered by Walsall Corporation, contrasts with veteran 1950 Guy Arabs drafted in from Birmingham. / *T. W. Moore*

Walsall contributed a very mixed fleet of buses and trolleybuses, although recent purchases had standardised on short length Daimler Fleetlines. West Midlands has the distinction of being the only PTE to operate trolleybuses, although their demise was regrettably made an early priority. The closure took place in October 1970 and marked the end of the country's penultimate system. The surviving trolleybus network, that of Bradford City Transport, closed before that undertaking was absorbed into a PTE.

West Bromwich had largely standardised on the Daimler CVG6, each painted in the traditional lined-out livery of cream and two shades of blue. The latest purchases were two batches of Daimler Fleetlines in a plain 'lowheight' livery of mainly cream. Like the other three operators, West Bromwich had a batch of Fleetlines on order at the time of absorption. These would have been normal height leaving one to wonder which livery they would have received.

Wolverhampton did not possess any rear-engined double-deckers although its first Fleetlines were on order. The newest buses were a small fleet of AEC Swifts and Daimler Roadliners. The vast majority of the fleet consisted of Guy Arabs, although some veteran Daimler CVG6s were also still working. Notable too was a pair of Guy Wulfrunians.

Steps towards integration were taken, such as the introduction of the Travelcard season ticket, but real advances could not be made until control was obtained of Midland 'Red' services within the West Midlands. The 'Red' services frequently operated in buffer zones between the former municipal operators or duplicated their services. The £3.6m takeover in December 1973 of appropriate services (and 413 buses) gave the green light for an integrated transport network. The buses included BMMO double- and single-deckers, Daimler Fleetlines, and small numbers of Leyland Leopards and Nationals.

The redrawing of local government boundaries led to the absorption of Coventry Corporation Transport on 1 April 1974. A fleet largely consisting of Daimler CVG6 and Fleetline models was handed over, bringing up the number of West Midlands PTE buses to the 2,600 mark.

The predominance of Daimler chassis and Gardner engines amongst acquired stock is striking and it is not surprising that the Gardner-engined Fleetline remained the PTE standard for the first 10 years. Difficulties in receiving sufficient numbers of the model led to other types entering the fleet however, eg Bristol VRs, Leyland-engined Fleetlines and Ailsas. Concern over step heights caused standardisation on rear-engined vehicles for the single-deck fleet too. In recent years this has automatically meant Nationals. The arrival of 'new era' double-deckers initially saw a splitting of orders between Metrobuses and Titans. One-man operation was extended rapidly, Birmingham being completed in October 1977 when the Outer Circle was converted and the last veteran Birmingham 'Standards' of 1950-4 withdrawn.

The PTE has vigorously followed its road/rail integration brief, feeding bus services to or past rail stations where appropriate. A feature of the Solihull revised network was the introduction of a Dial-a-Bus scheme, at first based on Knowle and Dorridge and later extended to Solihull. Dial-a-Bus succeeded in re-awakening public transport in an affluent area but the vehicles were too small ever to be profitable. The high spot of the road/rail policy was the introduction in May 1978 of the frequent 'Cross-City Line', virtually a new rail facility between Longbridge and Birmingham City Centre, linked across the City with the existing line to Four Oaks.

Left: This batch of 100 Guy Arabs with Metro-Cammell bodies, delivered to Birmingham City Transport in 1950-1, must have created a record for continuous service on heavy urban routes without rebodying or rebuilding when the last were withdrawn in October 1977. No 2624 was a Perry Barr garage contribution to service 92, then a cross-city service from Pheasey to Hall Green, when seen in Lower Bull Street in April 1975. / *MRK*

Below: 1953 Crossley-bodied Daimler CVG6 3110 heads a line of 'extras' waiting in Snow Hill, Birmingham, to clear the crowds for the West Bromwich Albion ground in September 1971. New Daimler Fleetline 4044, one of the first with Park Royal body to PTE standard, passes by on its left. / *MRK*

Above: No 3246 was one of the trial batch of 10 Daimler Fleetlines received by Birmingham City Transport early in 1962. This vehicle toured the country when new demonstrating to bus operators on behalf of the manufacturer. The batch carried Metro-Cammell bodies and was never converted to one-man operation. No 3246 passes a classic BCT bus stop plate as it climbs the Bull Ring in April 1975 — compare this scene with that showing trolleybus 76 on page 108. / *MRK*

Left: Body contracts of production BCT Fleetlines were split between Park Royal and Metro-Cammell. No 3414, built in 1964 with body by the former, loads outside Birmingham's impressive Council House, Victoria Square, in August 1977. Ex-BCT buses continued to be turned out with khaki roofs even after new vehicles and repaints in other divisions received cream. / *MRK*

SHOES
90
PHEASEY ESTATE
VIA KINGSTANDING
3467
PAY AS YOU ENTER
BON 467C

967
CASTLE VALE LIMITED STOP
PAY AS YOU ENTER
SANYO
ALISTS
JOL 654E

eft: In 1965, Birmingham took delivery f 24 Daimler Fleetlines with rather odd Marshall single-deck bodies. Several perators subsequently followed suit but sually avoided the sawn-off louble-decker look. No 3467 assists in Bull Street on the normally double-decked 0 service in August 1978. / *MRK*

Below left: More unusual single-deckers, t least for a municipal operator, ollowed in 1967 when 12 Ford R192s vith Strachans bodies were delivered for new limited stop service. No 3654 is een in Priory Circus in July 1977 on the ubsequently introduced Castle Vale imited stop facility. / *MRK*

Right: Walsall Corporation had been firm Dennis users before World War II, and he marque staged a comeback in the late ifties with the Loline. No 885, dating rom 1960, was the last to arrive and arried a Willowbrook body. It retained Valsall livery in October 1971. Walsall's us station has since been rebuilt. / *MRK*

Below: Passengers alight from the centre xit of former Walsall Daimler leetline 42L. Despite the two doors, Northern Counties managed to ccommodate 70 passengers in the short ength body. / *T. W. Moore*

Left: The BMMO D9s taken over from Midland Red are sadly missed. No 4981, dating from 1962, works the 'D&S' (Dudley and Stourbridge service) in April 1974. This particular stop on a sharp incline in Dudley bus station, defeated heavily laden Daimler CVG6s pressed into service as the D9s began to fade from the scene. / *MRK*

Below: The hard-pressed ex-Midland Red fleet at Dudley was supplemented by these 1960 Leyland Atlanteans, purchased from Kingston-upon-Hull in 1975. Roe-bodied 1153 overtakes 1145 with Metro-Cammell body in October 1975. / *T. W. Moore*

Right: The last of a trio of Park Royal-bodied AEC Reliances built for Wolverhampton Corporation in 1963 loads at Victoria Square bus station in that town. Behind, ex-Midland Red Leyland Leopard/Willowbrook 5201 arrives from Stourbridge in October 1974. / *T. W. Moore*

Below right: 1958 Daimler CVG6/Metro-Cammell 240Y, still in Coventry colours in Ironmonger Row during July 1978, was one of many similar buses then continuing to give good service. Prototype Birmingham Fleetline 3241, one of two transferred to Coventry in 1978, noses up behind. / *MRK*

57 BLOXWICH
256
707 CDA

HEAR AIDS
21
ALDERMAN'S GREEN
VWK 240

Above: 1964 Leyland Atlantean PDR1/2 342Y, with Willowbrook body, is dwarfed by the Coventry Theatre in May 1978. / *T. W. Moore*

Centre left: Now restored to reasonable tranquility since the opening of a bypass, Allesley village looks busy as buses create congestion in June 1975. 1966 Daimler Fleetline 6Y was one of the first batch taken by Coventry to feature East Lancs bodies. / *MRK*

Below left: Body contracts on early Coventry Fleetlines were varied. Willowbrook-bodied 365Y manoeuvres behind 34Y with Eastern Coach Works body in this excellent late evening shot of Pool Meadow in December 1977. / *T. W. Moore*

Above right: Two batches of Daimler Fleetlines were supplied to West Bromwich Corporation with low-height bodies for operation under a low bridge. They received a special livery and the PTE has continued this distinction by modifying its own layout. 1969 ECW-bodied 120H is not passing beneath the bridge concerned, however. British Rail kindly identifies the location in July 1976. / *T. W. Moore*

Right: The rolling stock from Walsall and the Wolverhampton garages was revolutionised by 200 Bristol VRTs with Metro-Cammell bodies delivered between 1973 and 1975. Prince Albert ignores 4644 being pursued by the mayoral car through Queen Square, Wolverhampton, in July 1976. / *T. W. Moore*

British Rail Oldbury
14'6"
19
OLDBURY
Hill Top
TEA 120G

501
TETTENHALL
PRIVATE
GOG 844N
ALBERT

Left: The 1967 ECW-bodied Bristol RESL6G single-deckers were virtually redundant in their city of origin, Coventry, when the PTE took over. They led a much travelled life within the PTE; 5519 was working from Stourbridge garage when seen at Dudley bus station in February 1977. / *MRK*

Left: Slow delivery of Fleetlines led to the purchase in 1976 of 50 Ailsa Volvos with Alexander bodies which followed three prototypes. Many went to Oldbury garage where 4752 is seen in July 1977 loading in the town's old bus station. / *MRK*

Left: Eight Ford/Alexander S midibuses introduced the Knowle and Dorridge Dial-a-Bus scheme in 1975. This was later extended to Solihull as indicated on the blue destination blind of No 4736, seen at Knowle bus shelter in July 1977. The Dial-a-Bus network, with its heavy overheads, was replaced by Hail-a-Bus in 1978. / *MRK*

Above: Senior citizens' free travel schemes are good business but can cause problems. West Midlands 159 service can suffer from overcrowding, particularly on summer Saturdays, as Birmingham pensioners take the scenic route via the Airport, National Exhibition Centre and Meriden to Coventry, which is developing as a tourist centre. 1976 Fleetline/Park Royal 6588 looks much in demand at Birmingham International station in August 1978. / *MRK*

Left: Fleetline 6722 is part of an order placed by Coventry, hence the East Lancs body. It was one of 20 initially operated from Acocks Green garage, Birmingham, before subsequent transfer to Coventry. No 6722 swings into Solihull station when new in July 1977. / *MRK*

Below left: Some West Midlands Leyland Nationals are finished to dual-purpose specification, and wear the special livery shown. No 6854 offers passengers on the Coventry station service considerable comfort as it pulls into the station when new in July 1978. / *MRK*

To close the book, views of the two biggest rivals for the PTE market. *Left:* West Midlands MCW Metrobus 6831 is another bus demonstrating the effectiveness of gritting crews. *Below:* Leyland Titan 7001 for the same operator looks immaculate before entering everyday service in 1978. Note the differing liveries. / *T. W. Moore; MRK*